Mrs. Kerby

BOYS' LIFE OF
JOHN F. KENNEDY

BOYS' LIFE OF JOHN F. KENNEDY

by Bruce Lee

New York

Distributed by

Sterling Publishing Co., Inc., New York

Third Printing, 1963

Copyright © 1961 by
Bold Face Books, Inc.
419 Park Avenue South, New York 16, N.Y.

Manufactured in the United States of America

Library of Congress Catalog Card No.: 61–15730

Acknowledgments

I WOULD like to thank the family of President John F. Kennedy and his hard-working White House staff without whose assistance this book would have been impossible to write. I am also indebted to the President's friends—LeMoyne Billings, his roommate at Choate and Princeton; Thomas Schriber, who was one of Joseph P. Kennedy, Jr.'s, closest friends from boyhood until Joe, Jr.'s tragic death; Charles Spaulding, who is one of the President's closest friends today and was invaluable in providing leads for tracking down obscure facts—and the President's coaches and teachers at Choate School.

Washington, D.C., Sept. 1961   Bruce Lee

Contents

PROLOGUE
The Inauguration (1961)

DESPITE the bitter, below-freezing temperature and a biting 40-mile-an-hour wind from the northwest, the ceremony was beautiful. The wooden stands and the dome of Washington's Capitol were flawlessly white in the brilliant winter sun. The sky was a deep, hurricane blue. The top hats and thick overcoats worn by dignitaries from all over the world were inky black, and wind-whipped banners gleamed red and white and blue. The setting was perfect, its technicolor perfection almost unreal.

There was the Marine Band, with its bright colors and regimental battle ribbons streaming in the wind, playing "America the Beautiful" and thumping out the national anthem. On the wooden stands an aging, mellowing President, Dwight D. Eisenhower, was turning over his burdens to a much younger man. A great political contest had ended, the reins of government were changing hands, and America was moving on. At 12:21 on the chilly afternoon of January 20, 1961, the presiding officer of the inauguration ceremonies solemnly intoned: "We are here to inaugurate the thirty-fifth president of this free people."

Moments later, John Fitzgerald Kennedy became, at

9

43, the youngest President ever elected to lead the United States of America. He stood up to a blare of fanfares, removed his black topcoat, paced forward to face Chief Justice of the United States Earl Warren, and over a closed, family Douay Bible, his breath frosty in the frigid air, raised his right hand and pronounced the majestic words that symbolized his taking office: "I do solemnly swear. . . ."

No matter what crises lay ahead, no matter what heartache, hard work, suffering and courage lay behind, this would remain the great moment in Jack Kennedy's life.

The new President's inaugural address became famous, moments after its delivery. Jack Kennedy talked not only to the people of America, but to the people of the world. In clear, clean language a new American President with a fresh and vigorous style beamed a message of hope to people everywhere.

"Let the word go forth from this time and place," declared young President Kennedy, "to friend and foe alike, that the torch has been passed to a new generation of Americans—born in this century, tempered by war, disciplined by a cold and bitter peace, proud of our ancient heritage—and unwilling to witness or permit the slow undoing of those human rights to which this nation has always been committed, and to which we are committed today." Strongly, Boston accent crackling through the frosty afternoon, right hand chopping the air, he continued: "Let every nation know, whether it wish us well or ill, that we shall pay any price, bear any burden, meet any hardship, support any friend or oppose any foe in order to assure the survival and success of liberty.

"This much we pledge—and more. . . ."

Jack Kennedy did not speak emptily. Although he was young compared to the statesmen around him, and though his bushy brown hair bristled over his forehead like that of a young boy's in desperate need of a haircut, the new President knew of what he spoke.

He was born to an era of depression and violence. He knew—because his father had been the American ambassador to Great Britain—the intricacies demanded by the art of diplomacy. He understood—because he had been a Congressman and a Senator for 14 years—the art of power politics. And, as well as any veteran—as the commander of torpedo boats in the South Pacific—he knew the horrors of war.

So when President Kennedy said, "My fellow Americans: Ask not what your country will do for you—ask what you can do for your country. My fellow citizens of the world: Ask not what America will do for you, but what together we can do for the freedom of man," he knew the sacrifice and hard work that lay behind his declaration.

Part One
THE EARLY YEARS

I
Jack and Joe

WHAT KIND of boy had this young President been?

The year is 1929. Here is the home of the Kennedy family, a huge Georgian mansion set on rambling acres in a very fashionable section of Bronxville, just north of New York City.

Inside, on the rug in the living room, two young boys are wrestling. The older boy, Joe, Jr., is 14, heavy-set and good-looking. The younger boy, John, called Jack by everyone, is 12, smaller and skinnier than his brother. Upstairs, on the staircase, six younger Kennedy children are watching the fight. Five of them are girls—Rosemary, Kathleen, Eunice, Pat and Jean. The youngest, 4 years old, is a boy—Bobby. In a few years, a ninth Kennedy child, Teddy, will arrive.

Joe will win the fight, he almost always does. He is older, heavier, stronger. But Jack is fighting ferociously, pummeling his older brother and being pounded in return. It is not an ordinary fight, for this is not an ordinary family. Moments later the fight ends and the older children, Joe and Jack included, for they are now best of pals again, will be playing a rugged, bone-

crushing game of touch football with some friends on
the large lawn outside.

Outside, the father, Joseph P. Kennedy Sr., will
watch the game, acting as his own private cheering
section whooping and hollering first for one side, then
the other. "Old Joe wouldn't play any of the games,"
one friend of the Kennedy children recalls. "He was
too smart for that."

Indeed, Joseph P. Kennedy is not an ordinary man
either. Just a little over 40 years of age, he is already a
self-made millionaire many times over. As the years
progress he will become one of the very wealthiest
men in the country. He is active in politics and will
hold high governmental positions. He made his early
fortune in Boston. As his business grew, he moved his
large family to New York in 1926 when Jack, his second oldest son, was ten. He is extraordinarily proud of
his growing children, he is interested in their welfare,
and anxious for their future.

Joe Kennedy's father, Patrick Kennedy, had fought
vicious anti-Irish prejudice in Boston and become the
political leader of East Boston. Joe Kennedy himself
has faced the hardship of being an Irish Catholic in
Boston. This, in fact, was one reason he had moved
his family to New York. One day he would be the
United States Ambassador to England. But what, he
mused to himself, would become of the fiery and aggressive band of children he was now watching on the
lawn? Whatever it would be, he would help them—not
by money, for already he could see that they would always have enough of that—but by instilling in them
the things that counted: courage, industry, ambition,
family loyalty, patriotism, firm religious beliefs, and
a love of competition.

The children's mother, Rose, is watching the game from a window in the house. She, too, is not an ordinary person. Gracious, cultured, efficient and beautiful, she is the daughter of John "Honey Fitz" Fitzgerald, one-time Mayor of Boston. Jack's earliest memories are of his very young childhood in Brookline, Massachusetts, touring the political wards with Grandfather Fitzgerald—then engaged in a tough campaign for Governor of Massachusetts. In later years, when Jack would run for office, one sly wit would say, "The Kennedys aren't really Democrats and they're certainly not Republicans—they're a political party unto themselves."

The firm discipline and love of competition that Joseph P. Kennedy instilled in his nine children was strong stuff. When the father was away from home for business or political reasons, the hand of authority was given to young Joe, Jr. who was as tough as his Dad.

So it came to be, in natural fashion, that Jack was the only real rival Joe had in the family; the other children close to them in age were girls; the younger boys were still small. And so the oldest sons, Joe and Jack, fought often and hard and long. Jack, being smaller, always seemed to come off second best.

The boys' father, of course, knew about this competition between his sons but he did little to stop it. For he knew that Joe, Jr. made up for his tough ways with unbounded generosity in helping his younger brothers and sisters. Today, Jack admits that despite his fights with his older brother, their friendship and their love for each other was deep. Jack still thinks highly and lovingly of his elder brother, but admits: "He had a pugnacious personality. Later on it smoothed out but it was a problem in my boyhood."

That the problem was painful is clear; no one likes
to be a consistent loser, and to a Kennedy, bred to be a
winner, losing was especially difficult. That losing
never became a habit to Jack is also clear, for his tough
spirit never broke, and he would doggedly test his bigger brother again and again. Victory, when it came,
was just that much tastier.

Victory and courage were the keystones of the philosophy that Joseph P. Kennedy passed along to his
children. Indeed, this was the code transmitted to him
by his father Patrick, who had skillfully clambered to
the top of Boston's political pile.

"Joe wanted his children to be thinkers and doers,"
recalls Tom Schriber, a close boyhood friend of Joe, Jr.
"He'd get them to sit down and he'd tell them, 'I don't
care what you do in life, but whatever you do, be the
best person in the world when you do it. Even if you're
going to be a ditch digger, be the best ditch digger in
the world.'"

The family did everything to introduce the children
to all forms of athletics. At the family's summer home
at Hyannis Port, at Cape Cod, Massachusetts, they had a
tennis court and facilities for sailing and swimming.
Even the girls learned to play a particularly wicked
game of touch football. Later on, though the girls might
shudder at the term "tomboy," they could still pass, and
kick and run almost as well as their brothers. Sometimes when their brothers had beaten them badly in a
vicious game of tennis, the girls would leave the tennis
court sobbing, only to return a little while later to try
and beat the boys. At the family's winter home in Palm
Beach, Florida, their father always had a professional
trainer on hand to make sure the children stayed in

top physical shape. The professional would make sure they swam so many laps in the pool, or did so many chin-ups, or brushed up on their boxing.

"They are the most competitive and at the same time the most cohesive family I've ever seen," said one family friend. "They fight each other, yet they feed on each other. They stimulate each other. Their minds strike sparks. Each of them has warm friends, but none they like and admire so much as they like and admire their own brothers and sisters."

One of the children's favorite pastimes was sailing. When they were small, everyone would go out together in a little sloop they named the "Tenofus." Later, after Teddy was born, the crowding became too much, and they purchased a larger boat that they called "Onemore." Characteristically, when Jack received his first boat, he named it "Victura." "It has something to do with winning," he explained when queried about the name.

"Neither Jack nor Joe feared anything," says one of their sailing friends. The two boys would go sailing on days when it was so rough you could barely see the boat between the waves. One classic voyage occurred when the waves were running so high that no other boat in the harbor dared to leave its mooring, but Joe, Jack and two friends went out for a wild wet ride. Joe and his friend, being in command of the situation, forced Jack and his friend to sit on the windward side of the boat where the waves drenched them constantly. It was a long sail, and both Jack and his companion were furious; but there was nothing they could do, so they suffered, though not in silence. Today, the memory of that sail remains fresh in their minds, and if it is a joking matter now, it wasn't at the time.

While Jack and his brother enjoyed themselves athletically, their father kept working on improving their minds. He would take the boys into the library of the Bronxville home and discuss the latest problems in the news. As the younger children grew older, their father moved the talks from the library to the dinner table, and soon, dinnertime became the hour for thoughtful and sometimes argumentative discussions of current events.

The family was rich, but both parents made a supreme effort to keep the children from being spoiled by money. "We tried to teach them never to waste an opportunity," explained Rose. "We never gave them allowances that were any bigger than those of the neighborhood children. We never put a value on anything just because it was expensive. Nobody talks about money in Boston, and we made it a rule never to speak about money in our house."

To prove their point, the Kennedys exhibit a letter Jack wrote asking for an increased allowance shortly after becoming a Boy Scout. His grammar was terrible, but he was able to get his message across.

"My recent allowance is 40¢," Jack started out by saying. "This I use for aeroplanes and other playthings of childhood but now I am a scout and I put away my childish things. Before I would spend 20¢ of 40¢ and in five minutes I would have empty pockets and nothing to gain and 20¢ to lose. When I am a scout I have to buy canteens, haversacks, blankets, searchlicgs, ponchos, things that will last for years and I can always use it while I can't use chocolate marshmallow sunday ice cream and so I put in my plea for a raise of thirty cents for me to buy schut things and pay my way around. . . ."

Only rarely was money used as a reward. Joe, Sr. exacted a firm pledge from each child not to smoke or drink until he or she reached 21 years of age. The incentive for keeping the promise was a bonus of $2,000, payable on the twenty-first birthday, which could be kept or returned according to whether or not the child had kept his promise.

The Kennedy policy of not talking about money was followed so closely that the parents didn't tell their children that when each one reached the age of 21, he or she would receive a trust fund of a million dollars. According to Rose Kennedy none of her children knew about this money until they read about it in a magazine.

It is interesting to note that while Joe Kennedy was stubborn and harsh in the heat of argument, he was adamant that his children should be financially independent and have the courage to make up their own minds. Talking of their trust funds, he says with pride: "I fixed it so that any of my children, financially speaking, could look me in the eye and tell me to go jump in the lake."

Jack moved steadily ahead, step by step through the fourth, fifth, and sixth grades of the near-by Riverdale Country School in the West Bronx. Occasionally his mother would drop in and chat with his teachers to see how he was progressing. Today, his teachers remember Jack as a slight, polite, serious boy, who loved history and had a hot temper.

"He had a quiet, studious childhood," says Rose reviewing her son's early accomplishments. "In fact, I think, in looking back, that he was the quietest of the children."

Quiet or not, Jack was capable of raising a ruckus. But childish pranks found little favor with his mother. "I'm a rather old-fashioned girl, and I believe in corporal punishment," says Rose Kennedy sternly, "and many's the slap I've given Jack and the others."

Rose Kennedy is deeply religious, and she instilled her beliefs in her children. Explaining her feelings on the subject, she says, "I don't know about religion as a national or a political issue, but I think religion is wonderful for children. Most children seek this stability and purpose, and religion has meant a lot in Jack's life."

Summing up the home life of the Kennedy children, Rose recently gave her reasons for the strong family solidarity of the Kennedys. "I suppose it's because of their home background," she says. "We have always been a very stable Catholic family, and my husband always took time to discuss things with the children, however heavy his political pressures.

"My husband was quite a strict father; he liked the boys to win at sports and everything they tried. If they didn't win, he would discuss their failure with them, but he did not have much patience with the loser."

Jack, as Rose remembers it, was the big reader among the children. She recalls that she rarely saw Jack by himself when he didn't have a book with him. Nothing made him happier than being first to get the newspaper. When he read, Rose recalls, he did it with complete concentration and would notice nothing else go-

ing on around him. His reading habits, and his love of
reading, would remain with Jack for the rest of his life.

In 1930, at the age of 13, Jack prepared to leave
home for the first time—he would soon start college
preparatory studies at Canterbury School in New Mil-
ford, Connecticut. Gone would be the constant near-
ness of the close-knit family circle that had meant so
much to him. His parents had believed that if the
older children were well-trained, they in turn would
teach the younger ones. And so, Joe and Jack taught
their younger brothers and sisters all they knew. In
doing so, both boys learned to love and appreciate the
younger children. Some older children regard the
younger ones as millstones around their necks; this
didn't occur with the Kennedy children. It would be
sad, Jack thought, to leave his wonderful family to
head for prep school.

II
Prep School

WITHIN a few months after entering Canterbury, Jack was over his initial feelings of loneliness. "I felt pretty homesick but it's O.K. now," he wrote home after he'd settled down to the school's routine.

Although he was a natural athlete, Jack encountered his first setback when he tried out for the football team and was turned down because he didn't weigh enough. Undaunted, he hunted around for another varsity sport and soon reported home that his swimming had improved to a point where he could cover 50 yards in half a minute.

Settling down to a strict schedule, he wrote his mother, "We have chapel every morning and evening and I will be quite pius I guess when I get home." But he had only moderate success with his grades and, as his letters indicate, spelling was not his strong point. At one time, Jack had serious trouble with his Latin studies, and his teacher commented on the report card, "He can do better than this."

Despite the problem with his grades, Jack kept abreast of current events. He wrote to his father asking him to send the *Literary Digest,* a political magazine of the early thirties.

24

When he applied himself, he showed a remarkable aptitude for remembering what he read. "We are reading 'Ivanhoe' in English," he wrote his father, "and though I might not be able to remember material things such as tickets, gloves and so on I can remember things like Ivanhoe and the last time we had an exam in it I got a 98."

When he returned home for Easter vacation, Jack was laid low by an attack of appendicitis, and was unable to finish the spring semester at Canterbury.

In the fall, Jack joined his older brother Joe, Jr. at Choate preparatory school, also in Connecticut, and one of New England's finest private schools. Significantly, Choate was not a Catholic school as Canterbury had been. Jack's switch to Choate firmly established the pattern of education Joe, Sr. had in mind for his children; the girls would attend Catholic parochial schools, the boys would go to secular schools. Their father's reasoning was simple. Already he saw that the boys might one day enter politics—at a nonparochial school they would have an opportunity to meet a wider cross section of friends. Although Choate was not a Catholic school, the boys kept up their religious obligations and, in long letters home, constantly reported on what they were doing.

Joe was well ahead of Jack in school. The older boy began making a name for himself as a top athlete as soon as he arrived at Choate. Jack, lighter and smaller, found himself unable to compete with his brother on the varsity level. But he loved athletics and entered the intramural leagues where he played against boys his own size with a tiger-like ferocity.

"The most burning thing I can remember about Jack

was that he was a fighter," Jack's football coach remembers with pride. "You take Joe, he was a real athlete. But Jack made up for what he lacked in athletic ability with his fight."

Jack was lazy in practice but not when the chips were down. The coach would try to speed up football signal drills by running along behind the boys, and, if he could catch them, he'd wallop them to make them run faster. But he could never catch Jack. "Jack would lope along and when I'd get close he'd put on an extra burst of speed and leave me behind," his coach remembers with a laugh. "He was terribly fast. I could run 100 yards in 11 seconds, but he could beat me."

Young Kennedy's main failings were scholastic. His grades were well above average in English and history, but he had trouble with languages—especially Latin. Biology and chemistry bored him. Consequently, he found himself in trouble several times. "Jack only applied himself with average effort so he only got average grades," one teacher remembers. "I used to talk with him regularly. He'd promise to do better, but the results were not forthcoming; he was just like all the other boys his age. We'd have conferences every two weeks about his grades. Sometimes he'd need them, sometimes he wouldn't."

Jack's classmates agree with this evaluation. "He didn't work very hard," one friend says. His roommate LeMoyne Billings, summed it up this way: "The difference between Jack then and today is that today, if he found he was weak in some particular field, he'd work at it to better himself."

As the years passed, Jack grew taller and handsomer and more sure of himself. The strong family bonds remained, but also growing was a deep sense of individuality, a self-awareness. He was Jack Kennedy—with certain talents, certain failings, certain interests. The key to his life, Jack began to realize, was to exploit his talents and interests and to conquer his failings as best he could. It was a process of growth, and as Jack matured he found that his interests and talents were many. "He was one of the most versatile people I've ever seen," Billings says. "If there was anything going on, he was in on it."

Still, Jack found time to subscribe to *The New York Times* and wade through its weighty contents every day. The interest in international affairs instilled in Jack by his father would never flag. "He didn't just buy the paper to read the sports pages and comics," says an acquaintance.

Jack dressed informally. Khaki pants, heavy sweaters, white buck shoes were his general daytime wear. In the evening the boys had to wear coats and ties for dinner and the regular informal chapel service before study hall. Despite the casual air he maintained, Jack was conscious of his failings. He was aware his father wanted him to do well, but he found it difficult to sit down and apply himself to courses that didn't interest him. "If it were not for Latin," he once wrote his mother, "I would probably lead the lower school, but I am flunking that by ten points." Again he wrote, "Maybe Dad thinks I am alibing but I am not. I have been doing a little worrying about my studies because what he (father) said about starting off great and then going down sunk in."

When he wanted to, Jack could call upon tremendous powers of concentration. "If he was absorbed in reading a book," Lem Billings remembers, "you could talk to him and he wouldn't even know you were in the room."

There were many evenings when Jack would visit brother Joe for a long bull session. The boys would talk about anything that came to mind—how they disliked the school's strict discipline, what chances Choate stood in the next football game with a rival school, and, naturally enough, girls.

By now, Joe and Jack had formed a warm bond of affection. The rivalry of old had been largely replaced by understanding. There were certain differences in their abilities and personalities to be sure: Jack wanted to be as good an athlete as Joe, but Jack's light physique prevented that. Joe was bluff and hearty; Jack was quieter but formed deeper friendships. The friends and teachers of both boys disclaim the existence of any serious conflict between the two during the years at Choate.

"The rivalry between Jack and Joe has been overplayed," a former classmate says today. "If you say Jack wasn't as outgoing as Joe, that just isn't so. Jack had more friends, more intimate friends than Joe ever did. Jack was much more of an extrovert despite what people say. It was Joe who was very hard to get to know."

Tom Schriber, one of Joe's closest boyhood friends, backs this up. "Sure I think Jack had something of a complex about Joe in those early years," he says, "but it was largely the feelings of a younger brother toward an older brother. Joe matured very early, Jack improved himself as he grew up. Joe was a year or so older and Jack couldn't overcome this edge, but still, they were as close as two brothers could possibly be. And I think that if Joe was alive today, Jack would have passed him as a politician. This showed up pretty early. Jack was willing to compromise. Joe never would. . . .

"Sure the two of them would fight. It was serious, yes, but they were never out to hurt each other. Usually they'd get in a hassle at home because Joe would want to take the boat one place and Jack would want to take it another. So they'd fight. Joe was bigger, and he'd win and take the boat. But then Jack would go along with him, just as happy as can be."

Tom Schriber also recalls that the brothers did more than just sail together. Under the expert guidance of their father they were learning to think in a reasoned and logical manner about important issues of the day. Schriber remembers one scene in the high-ceilinged book-lined library of the Bronxville home during school vacation. Joe Kennedy Sr., Jack, Joe, Jr., and Schriber were present. Father Kennedy started talking about the Civilian Conservation Corps, a new youth program President Roosevelt had just initiated to help combat the depression. Quickly and intensely the Kennedy boys jumped into the discussion and explored the subject from every angle. For over an hour, the new CCC was the topic, and by the time the teenagers left the library they were at least as well informed about the subject as most adults—probably more so in fact.

After the discussion, recalls Schriber, the boys went out on the huge lawn of the house. Jack and some of the younger Kennedy brothers and sisters quickly challenged Joe, Jr., and Schriber to a game of touch football.

Describing the bedlam that surrounded the activity to a reporter, Schriber said, "There'd be children hanging all over us. We were older and stronger than they

were and so we won a lot. But there were more of them
than there were of us and you could never tell what
was going to happen. You had to remember there were
a lot of trees around the lawn at Bronxville. I always
ran looking for the trees and the ball at the same time.
But Joe and Jack and Bobby never did and WHANG!
that was that. They were always knocking themselves
out. I can remember many occasions when one or the
other of the boys would be picked up unconscious;
they were always bandaged and bruised all over."

By the time their senior year rolled around, Jack and
his roommate, LeMoyne Billings, decided that their
plain, wood-and-plaster room should be used for more
serious purposes than just skylarking, and Jack wrote
his father that he and Lem had talked seriously about
improving their poor grades. "We have definitely decided to stop fooling around," he wrote. "I really do
realize how important it is that I get a good job done
this year, if I want to go to England. I really feel, now
that I think it over, that I have been bluffing myself
about how much real work I have been doing." Jack's
marks improved almost overnight. (He received the
promised trip to England as a reward.)

But the driving force behind Jack's suddenly improved grades was not the simple promise of a trip
abroad or other material gains for a job well done. His
father took time out from his own busy schedule to
write, "Now, Jack, I don't want to give the impression
that I am a nagger, for goodness knows, that is the
worst thing a parent can be. After long experience in
sizing up people I definitely know you have the goods
and you can go a long way. Now aren't you foolish not
to get all there is out of what God has given you?

"After all," his father continued, "I would be lacking even as a friend if I did not urge you to take advantage of the qualities you have. It is very difficult to make up fundamentals that you have neglected when you were very young, and that is why I am urging you to do the best you can. I am not expecting too much, and I will not be disappointed if you don't turn out to be a real genius, but I think you can be a really worthwhile citizen with good judgment and understanding. . . ."

In this wise and understanding fashion Joe Kennedy, Sr. helped his children through school. "The greatest thing about Jack's father was his closeness with the children," a friend says. "They couldn't be what they are today without the help he gave them. But the remarkable thing was that he never pushed or pulled. It must have been a difficult thing for him not to give them too much and spoil them."

As a senior at Choate, Jack played a lot of golf, a strong game of tennis and rowed on the junior crew. He was 18 years old, lean, tall, handsome, intelligent and widely respected by his classmates.

Although some people remember Jack as a quiet boy, close friends from his Choate days recall him somewhat differently. "There was no question that Jack was outspoken, nor was he very tactful," one friend says. "He had a quick temper, but he never held any grudges. He'd explode one minute and forget it the next. He certainly wasn't all sugar and cream."

Jack was beginning to see that success, in anything, involved two things: ability and hard work. He had the ability, he knew. He was just learning how to apply himself to the hard work.

As a senior, his marks climbed and he was accepted by Princeton University as a freshman. Also accepted at

Princeton was his Choate roommate, Lem Billings.
Brother Joe, Jr. was at Harvard, where earlier in the century, Joe, Sr. had attended college. Jack, flush with his
new independence, planned to strike out on his own
at Princeton.

In the late spring of 1935 Jack was graduated from
Choate. Prophetically, his class voted him the person
"most likely to succeed."

Two early photos of John F. Kennedy. At right: about age 7. Below: aged 8 as a student in Dexter School, Brookline, Mass.

In 1928, aged ten, Jack Kennedy was a member of the first football team of the Dexter School in Brookline, Mass. The Kennedy family moved to Bronxville, N. Y. before Jack was able to graduate from Dexter.

Eight of the nine Kennedy children pose for a family portrait at their Hyannis Port summer home. Jack is second from right. At his left is older brother Joe.

1934: The Kennedy family. From left: Edward, Jean, Robert, Patricia, Eunice, Kathleen, Rosemary, John, Rose and Joseph Sr. Oldest son Joseph Jr. not in the picture.   *U.P.I.*

All eleven Kennedys.

Ambassador Joseph P. Kennedy and his 21-year-old son John.

U.P.I.

Back row, third from left: Jack Kennedy as a member of the Harvard swimming team.

1937: Joseph P. Kennedy seated at left. On arm of chair is Patricia, 13; behind her is Jack, 20. Seated at her father's feet is Jean, 9, and behind Jean is Eunice, 16. With Mrs. Kennedy (extreme right) are Joe Jr., 22, Rosemary, 19, Robert, 12 (next to fireplace) and Kathleen, 17, seated next to Edward, 6.   *U.P.I.*

Ambassador Kennedy and his two oldest sons: Joe Jr. (left) and Jack (right).

London, March 1939: Jack and Ambassador Kennedy leave
Croydon Airport for Rome where the elder Kennedy will
represent President Franklin Roosevelt at the coronation of
Pope Pius XII.   *U.P.I.*

PT-Boat skipper Jack Kennedy at a base in the South Pacific.

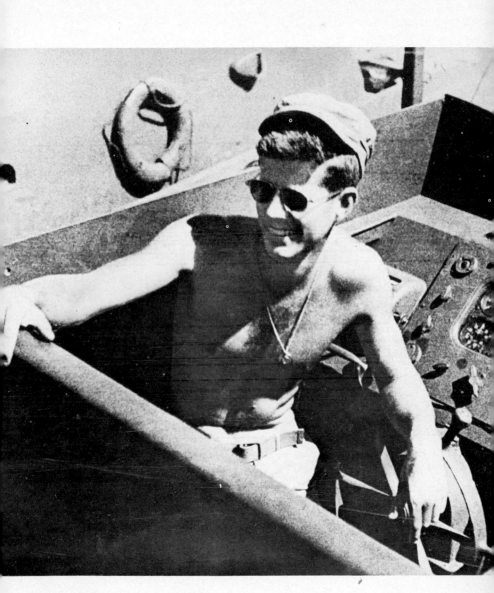

At the helm of PT-Boat 109.

The crew of PT-Boat 109. Skipper Kennedy is at far right.

A replica of the PT-109 passes the Presidential reviewing
stand at the Inauguration in 1961.

U.S. Army photo

Joseph Kennedy Jr. shortly before his death.

A war hero returns. Jack Kennedy at a war bond rally in Massachusetts.

1944: Lieutenant Kennedy is congratulated by Capt. F. L. Conklin in Boston after being awarded the Navy-Marine Corps medal for gallantry in action in the South Pacific.

The first political campaign—Boston, 1946. Twenty-eight-year-old Jack Kennedy talks to a women's group.

Kennedy poses happily with his parents and grandparents, Mr. and Mrs. John F. Fitzgerald during the 1946 campaign. Fitzgerald, called "Honey Fitz," was once Mayor of Boston.

1952: Renewed back trouble forces Kennedy onto crutches during his tough campaign for Senator in 1952.

Senator-elect Kennedy greets his supporters after the hectic 1952 race.

After the celebration—some serious words to the press. (1952)

III

The Depression

In October, 1929, when young Jack Kennedy was 12 years old and not yet in prep school, the United States was hit by a stock market "crash" that began on a day now known on Wall Street as "Black Friday."

In the months that followed, personal fortunes worth millions upon millions of dollars were wiped out; banks collapsed and went out of business. Some Wall Street speculators, rather than face the horror of going broke, committed suicide. Untold thousands of small investors—the everyday working man, the bootblack, the housewife, the farmer, the doctor—saw their life's savings turn to dust. Suddenly it no longer mattered how much stock anybody owned. The stocks seemed worthless, and millions of people found themselves unemployed.

Today, it's difficult to understand the terror that gripped the country in the depression years following the 1929 crash. Hungry people stood in line for hours, waiting for a free bowl of soup and an apple at relief kitchens hastily set up in vacant lots. The man holding a job that paid only a few dollars a week was considered lucky. It was a time of despair for most people.

The depression, however, did not affect Joseph P.

49

Kennedy, Sr. and his family. Only a month before the crash, in August of 1929, he suddenly took all of his money out of the stock market. At that time, the move seemed ill-advised. Stocks were going still higher and new fortunes were being made every day. When the bubble burst and other investors were wiped out, Joe found himself sitting pretty.

Years later, Joe explained his withdrawal from the market to reporters. As he told it, one day he was walking down Wall Street and dropped in at a shoeshine parlor. The boy shining his shoes didn't know him. "He looked up at me as he snapped the cloth over my shoes, and told me what was going to happen to various stocks and offerings on the market that day," Joe said.

The boy wasn't looking for a tip on the stock market, nor was he trying to impress Joe with his knowledge. He was just talking casually about what was going to happen. "I listened as I looked down at him," Joe continued, "and when I left the place, I thought: When the time comes that a shoeshine boy knows as much as I do about what is going on in the stock market, tells me so, and is entirely correct, there is something wrong either with me or with the market and it's time for me to get out. And I did."

As the 1920's became the 1930's, the country was in dreadful shape, but Joe Kennedy was doing fine. He had a sizable fortune, time on his hands, and politics in his blood. He also had a friend whose star was rising in the political field, Franklin D. Roosevelt.

In 1932 Roosevelt was nominated by the Democratic Party for the Presidency of the United States and Joe Kennedy was one of his staunchest supporters.

"I'm the only man with more than $12 who's for Roosevelt," Joe would say laughingly to friends, and in many respects he was right. The Republicans and many wealthy people feared Roosevelt, and hated him for his "New Deal" program to reconstruct the economy. But Joe agreed with Roosevelt's plans and he contributed $10,000 to the Democratic candidate's campaign funds.

In November, 1932, while Jack was at Choate, Roosevelt was elected President. He was inaugurated in March, 1933. One year after taking office, Roosevelt asked his friend, Joe Kennedy, to become Chairman of the Securities and Exchange Commission—a new federal agency that was to help rebuild and police the stock market.

Many people thought Roosevelt was wrong in naming tycoon Joe Kennedy as the man to police Wall Street. Newspapers ran violent editorials against Joe; Wall Street financiers ranted about the appointment over their luncheons at the Exchange Club. But they could not deny that the crash had left a stain on Wall Street's name. The market needed a strong set of rules that would restrain the speculators, frauds, cheats, and unscrupulous salesmen who sold worthless stocks to an unknowing public. And Joe Kennedy, who had operated as a lone wolf when the market was at its wildest, knew his way around such deadfalls, and understood every trick of the unscrupulous promoters and pool operators.

Joe tore into Wall Street's problems with a violence that stunned the nation. He prosecuted fraudulent stock operations from coast to coast, cleaning out pockets of greedy promoters with the instincts of an experienced hunter. Within six months, he made great strides toward building up the nation's confidence in Wall Street. When Joe took office, only $1 million worth of new securities were being put on the market each month. A little more than a year later, some $235 million worth of new issues were being offered each month, and Joe felt he had done his job.

Just 431 days after taking office, Joe decided to quit and move on to more challenging fields. Soon, Roosevelt named him to head the Maritime Commission, and again Joe Kennedy turned in a fine job.

So, when teen-aged Jack Kennedy at Choate School in Connecticut would look at *The New York Times* every day, there were many occasions when he could read of the latest exploits of his hard-driving father. This, of course, served to intensify Jack's interest in economic and political affairs.

Off in the not too distant future waited another important government post for Joseph P. Kennedy. When this one came, Jack would not just read about it—he would be directly involved.

IV
Harvard

BEFORE Jack went away to college, his father wanted
him to visit London during the summer to study at the
London School of Economics under the world-famous
socialist professor Harold Laski. And so, fresh from
Choate, the wiry, tall, 18-year-old youth set out for
Europe and a new world.

It was Joe Kennedy's belief that his boys would gain
greatly by studying in England under Laski and Joe,
Jr., had done this the summer before. Although Joe, Sr.
was not a socialist by a long shot, he knew that Laski
had a keen mind and that the Kennedy boys would
benefit from exposure to beliefs that differed from their
own. In a similar gesture, he later saw to it that both
boys had an opportunity to see Russia and the communist system.

In London, Jack found himself challenging many
new concepts, and rubbing shoulders with a broad
group of his fellow men. There, Jack met scholars, revo-
lutionaries, economists and writers from all parts of the
then far-flung British Empire.

Unfortunately, Jack wasn't able to benefit as fully
from these experiences as had his brother Joe, who, the
year before, had won the praise of the hard-bitten Laski

53

for his quick understanding of economic affairs. Jack
fell ill with jaundice and had to leave the London
School, remaining on the sick list until shortly after the
school year started at Princeton.

When he was finally able to enter college, Jack was
thrilled by Princeton's magnificent campus. He hurried
to get settled with his roommates, Lem Billings and
Ralph Horton, Jr., and catch up on his classes. Rather
than room in one of the fancy dormitories, which he
could very well afford, Jack chose to stay with Billings
and Horton who were not so well-off financially. The
three set up house in South Reunion Hall, where the
bathroom was in the cellar and the freshmen had to
scramble up and down seventy-five stairs to get to
their bedroom.

Only two months later, just as everything was going
well, Jack fell ill with jaundice once again. There was
little else to do but withdraw from Princeton. He did,
and spent the major part of the winter trying to regain
his health in Arizona. That fall, rather than go back
to Princeton and start out again, a full year behind his
friends, Jack decided to switch to Harvard where his
brother was finishing up.

So, in September of 1936, Jack returned to Boston,
the city of his birth. It had been ten years since the
Kennedy family had moved from Brookline, Mass., a
Boston suburb, to Bronxille, N.Y., a suburb of New York
City.

When Jack Kennedy started out at "The Yard," as
Harvard's campus is called, his goals were little changed
from those he had pursued years before at Choate.

Athletics were his primary interest. He tried out for
as many teams as he possibly could—football, swim-

ming, golf—and made the freshman team, though never
the first string, in all three sports. It was on the football
field that he first won the respect of his future roommate
Torbert H. "Torby" Macdonald, later an All-American
halfback on the Harvard eleven.

Doggedly determined to make first-string end on the
freshman football team, Jack would get Macdonald to
stay after practice and throw passes to him until it became too dark to see the darting football. But though
he impressed Macdonald with his aggressiveness, and
though Harvard's freshman football coach granted that
Jack was the best pass-catcher on the team, he was
underweight, and was cut from the varsity.

Kennedy refused to be upset by this lack of weight.
Rather than mope about it, or undertake some easier
sport, he boldly joined the junior varsity, and his aggressive play there led to another setback—a serious
back injury that in later life would almost kill him.
Blithely, he shrugged off the injury.

Jack's determination to do well was all-consuming.
He sought a position on the Harvard swimming squad as
a backstroker. But a week before a big race was to take
place, he came down with a serious attack of flu and was
hospitalized in the Harvard infirmary.

Jack was afraid that the infirmary's bland diet (his
favorite college meal was creamed soup, roast beef or
steak, potatoes, buttered carrots, ice cream and milk)
wouldn't give him enough energy to swim. So Jack
asked Macdonald to smuggle him steaks and malted
milks to keep up his strength. Then, with his roommate's
help, he would sneak out of the infirmary in the after-
noons, and, in spite of a high fever, practice swimming
in the pool when no one else was around.

Despite these elaborate schemes, Jack failed to win

a berth on the starting team. His place for the big race was taken by a classmate, Richard Tregaskis, who later became a famous war correspondent and wrote the blood-chilling book, *Guadalcanal Diary*.

Jack's swimming coach, Harold Ulen, vividly remembers the youth who tried so hard to make the team. "He was a fine kid, frail and not too strong, but always giving it everything he had," Ulen recalls. "He was more of a team man than an individualist and, in fact, was so modest he used to hide when news photographers would come around to take pictures of the team.

"Sometimes, if I put the stop watch on him for a sprint and his time didn't satisfy him, he'd get a little depressed, but that's all. He was the kind who'd bounce right back strong."

As Joe and Jack grew older, the differences between them became more noticeable. At Harvard, Joe showed he was a natural student. He could wait until the end of the term when exams were just a few days away, and then bone up on the subject overnight and pass his tests with flying colors. Jack, on the other hand, had to work for his grades; despite his fine memory, they didn't come easily. Joe was excitable—once, he started a fight because a Harvard classmate made snide remarks about former Boston Mayor John F. Fitzgerald without realizing that Joe was Fitzgerald's grandson. Jack, on the other hand, was cool, and was learning to approach problems from every angle—to study, to consider, and then follow through on a course of carefully planned action.

Despite their differences, Jack did many of the same things that Joe had done before him. It wasn't a case of

follow-the-leader; the two young men were sincerely
interested in many of the same things. Politics, for example, was in the blood of both Kennedys. Joe's more
rigid personality, however, led him along a narrower
political path than the one Jack followed. Jack learned
early that there are two sides to a story and that the
truth usually lies somewhere in between.

During his first two years at Harvard, Jack did only
fairly in his studies. His marks were "gentleman's
C" in most courses, and a C average at Harvard was
only good enough to squeak by and keep him out of
trouble with the dean's office.

Yet his latent ability didn't escape his professors'
keen eyes and one of them wrote at the time: "Kennedy's preparation may be spotty, but his general ability should bolster him up. He is surprisingly able when
he gets down to work. A commendable fellow."

During this period, the Harvard campus was seething
with unrest. Much of it stemmed from the depression
and President Roosevelt's New Deal reforms that were
beginning to be felt throughout the nation. Moreover,
there was trouble afoot in the world and an excited
student body kept a close watch on a new threat to
world freedom: German Nazism and its menacing
leader, Adolf Hitler.

Small clubs devoted to one political cause or another
spread across the campus. There were left-wing groups,
right-wing groups and middle-of-the-road groups, but
all were feverish in their interest. Students staged pa-
rades expressing their indignation about world events—
sometimes they were even thrown in jail for disturbing the peace. It was a time when the country's youth

was torn between past and present. If the past had been bad, they felt, the present was worse, and the future might be calamitous.

It is strange, therefore, that Jack Kennedy didn't become involved in any of these new-born student protest groups. But he didn't, and as historian James Mac-Gregor Burns succinctly pointed out, "What young Kennedy did *not* do at Harvard was more significant than what he did do."

Jack confined his activity to the more traditional activities at Harvard; he won a position on the *Harvard Crimson,* the college's influential student newspaper, joined the St. Paul's Catholic Club, and Hasty Pudding (a social club that presents an annual musical comedy throughout the country during Christmas vacations), and became a member of one of the college's exclusive eating clubs.

"Jack had the ability to be part of many different groups with varying interests," was the way Kennedy's roommate explained Jack's campus activities. "He was equally at home with the athletic crowd and the more intellectual group at the *Crimson.* He had the ability to share in a wide range of interests, without getting tied to one narrow group."

Jack was well-liked by his classmates and never displayed any sign of being spoiled because of his wealth and position as a famous man's son. His roommate, Torby Macdonald, was the son of a high school teacher, but differences of wealth never seemed to make any difference to either boy. In truth, the room Jack and Torby shared usually looked as though a cyclone had blown through it. They both followed the simple routine of dressing in whatever they first saw on the clothes pile in the morning. Inevitably, this was a baggy tweed jacket, khaki trousers and loafers.

"One time Jack was changing his clothes to go out," Macdonald delights in telling friends, "and he was heaving the clothes he was taking off into a pile in the middle of the floor. I told him to watch the way he was throwing things around our room because it was getting to look like a rummage sale.

" 'Don't get sanctimonious,' Jack said to me. 'Whose stuff do you think I'm throwing mine on top of—yours!' We never mentioned the subject again."

When Jack passed his twenty-first birthday, he inherited a trust fund of one million dollars, but no one at Harvard heard anything about it.

In fact, on one occasion, when he and Torby took their girl friends to dinner at an expensive Boston restaurant they discovered, to their horror, that they couldn't pay the bill. Jack, now a millionaire, had no money with him at all. His roommate had only eight dollars, not quite enough to cover the check. The two embarrassed boys had to borrow from their dates to avoid washing dishes to pay the bill.

V

Turmoil in Europe

WHILE Jack was at Harvard, his father's political star was rising. As the year 1937 drew to a close, President Roosevelt appointed Joe Kennedy as Ambassador to Great Britain, a post coveted by everyone in the diplomatic field. Two former Presidents of the United States, James Monroe and John Quincy Adams, had held the post. Among the other Americans who had served in the same role were men such as John Jay, Edward Everett, and James Russell Lowell. Now, with war clouds beginning to form over Europe, the English ambassadorial post was as important as it had ever been.

Many old-time Bostonians were profoundly upset by the appointment. They had never accepted the Boston Irish as equals and they were disturbed that Roosevelt would have the audacity to appoint a Boston Irishman to the Court of St. James's. The Ambassador to England is close to the very top of the social structure in both the old and new worlds and for Joseph Kennedy it was a subtle revenge—the immigrant had finally surpassed the blue bloods of Boston.

Shifting the Kennedy family to London brought special problems. The seven youngest children had to be

taken out of their American schools and transferred
to new ones in England.

Soon, under the gracious guidance of Rose Kennedy,
the embassy in London became just another household,
and the Kennedys, having already lived in Boston,
Washington, New York and other places, adjusted to
the change easily. The family quickly became truly international. Trips back and forth across the Atlantic became commonplace as did short sojourns at the new
Kennedy summer villa in Cannes on the French Riviera.

All this didn't mean the children didn't have problems. During the summer vacation of 1938 when Jack
and Joe made their first trip to visit their father at the
embassy, Jack was 21 and somewhat overwhelmed by
the impressive international circle of friends and associates in which his family now moved.

One day, Joe and Jack cornered one of their younger
sisters who had been in England for some time and made
her promise that she would get them invited to a British
debutante's coming-out party. An invitation was soon
forthcoming to a dance in one of London's swankiest
town houses.

No sooner had the two Kennedy brothers arrived,
than Jack spotted a beautiful girl with whom he wanted
to dance. Following American tradition, Jack started
to cut in on the young lady when a domineering young
British nobleman clapped him on the shoulder.

"Just a moment, my good chap," said the Britisher.
"You'll dance when it's your turn." What Jack hadn't
known was that the English custom decreed that men at
coming-out parties were supposed to obtain a number
and wait their turn to dance with one of the young
ladies.

It wasn't until 2 A.M. that Jack and Joe were able to

have their first dance. "To make matters worse," said
Jack later as he laughed about the mix-up, "they sicked
the two plainest-looking girls there on us. That was
enough for us Kennedys."

Returning to Harvard in the fall of 1938 Jack spent
the winter reading in the newspapers of the grim pre-
lude to war occurring in Europe. In September, part of
Czechoslovakia was given to Germany in a gesture of
appeasement by British Prime Minister Neville Chamberlain. There could be little doubt now that Hitler was
planning to conquer Europe—all of Europe. Farsighted
American businessmen were already leaving the Continent to return home, and this, of course, increased the
work load of the American embassies in Europe. Reading the letters from his father that told of the problems
facing the embassy staff, Jack grew more and more excited. He chafed at not being able to watch with his
own eyes the turmoil spreading through Europe. After
all, he was studying history and government and politics, and here was a golden opportunity to view these
subjects firsthand. Marshaling all his arguments, he
persuaded the Harvard authorities to let him spend the
second half of his junior year in Europe. In March of
1939, while Nazi troops were occupying Czechoslovakia, Jack crossed the Atlantic to join his father.

It was an exciting time. Jack was 22, handsome, able
and alert. Here, spread before his curious mind, was
the picture of a world going mad. Leading the parade
was a genius of a madman, Hitler. Madder still was the
idea that no one was doing anything effective to stop
the madness. Aside from its grim reality in terms of human lives, the situation was a once-in-a-lifetime spectacle for a fledgling student of political science such as

Jack Kennedy. When he joined his father in London, he realized gleefully that he would have an opportunity not only to observe the situation, but to take a diplomatic part in it as well.

Jack's arrival gladdened his father. Long before, Ambassador Kennedy had decided that to perform his duties well, he must report the current events in Europe to Washington in complete detail. He needed, as they say in the newspaper business, good "legmen," roving reporters and correspondents who had both sharp eyes and ears. His two sons, Joe, Jr., and Jack proved to be remarkably well-suited as correspondents.

In London, in 1939, Jack received a briefing from his father and immediately went to spend the spring in Paris, where he worked under the direction of Ambassador William Bullitt. Some of his missions were important, others were of a more routine nature. In the spring and summer he visited Poland, Russia, Turkey, and Palestine.

During these trips, Jack sent back to his father detailed reports of everything he saw and experienced. After every stop, the young man would sit down and mail his father a summation of the situation as he saw it. His reports contained an amazingly cool and objective view of the different situations and were of great value to Ambassador Kennedy.

With a newspaperman's instinct for reporting a situation thoroughly, Jack talked with representatives of diverse governmental groups in order to get both sides of the story. While in Warsaw, for example, he saw both journalists and diplomatic personnel plus "plenty of Poles, rich and poor," in his effort to understand the dispute brewing between the Poles and the Germans over the status of the small border state of Danzig. His report to his father carried a strong conclusion. "Probably the strongest impression I have gotten is that rightly or wrongly the Poles *will fight* over the question of Danzig," he wrote. Not too many months later, Jack's judgment was shown to be correct.

In Russia, Jack got a firsthand glimpse of communist life. A sleeping industrial giant, Russia had barely begun its first steps forward. As young Jack later recalled, the Soviet Union was a "crude, backward, hopelessly bureaucratic country."

Jack also visited the Crimean Peninsula and then took a ship for a visit to Istanbul. From there he went to Jerusalem, and sent his father a report about the touchy British-Arab-Jewish relations, basically agreeing with British policy.

In all, it was a heady time for Jack. The complex interplay of international politics left an indelible mark on his mind. The issues were vital ones that affected lives of countless millions of people, he realized. A person who could think clearly and help to negotiate disputes was performing a vital and useful service.

That Jack was beginning to see both the importance and fascination of the science of government is clearly demonstrated by a story told by Louella Hennessey, a long-time nurse for the entire Kennedy family. Jack, according to Miss Hennessey, stopped in during the summer at the family summer home in Cannes on the Riviera. On a stormy afternoon, in front of a crackling fire in the huge fireplace, Jack gathered his younger brothers and sisters before him and began telling them stories to while away the rainy hours. They were not ordinary stories, however, that young Jack related to the children whom he loved tenderly. Instead Jack told them the story of the rise and fall of the great nations and leaders of the world—starting with Hannibal, then Caesar, then Charlemagne, then Napoleon and finally bringing his enraptured audience up to the present. In detail, Jack explained that many of the great nations of the past were dictatorships that oppressed the people and these nations eventually were toppled. Now, Jack said, America will become the world's most powerful force, because she does not oppress her people. The great problem, Jack concluded, would be how to maintain America's power and also her tradition of individual freedom. It was *the* problem of our future, he said.

Vividly and dramatically Jack told the story. Even Teddy, then only six, listened intently through the whole narrative as told by a young man who would one day be called upon to solve just the problem that he was now beginning to perceive.

There were, of course, lighter moments for young Jack during these months. Jack's roommate, Torby Macdonald, had come to Europe during summer vacation time, and the two boys decided to drive from Paris to the Riviera for a party. Setting off, they crammed themselves into the front seat of a rented jalopy that was on its last legs.

Jack, who was driving as fast as he could, suddenly felt the wheel give a strong jerk to the right and the car headed for the edge of the road, teetered for a long instant, and then slid off on the right shoulder. The car turned over, skidded along on its top for about 30 feet, and finally came to a halt upside down.

As Macdonald relates it, "We were literally standing on our heads in the overturned car, when Jack looked

sidewise at me and said in a casual tone, 'Well, pal, we
didn't make it, did we?' "

For every lighthearted incident, however, there
were others that were covered with the grime of a sick
continent. Once, in Munich, Jack's careful diplomatic
consideration of a dangerous moment saved himself,
Macdonald, and another All-American halfback, Byron
"Whizzer" White, from what could have been an ugly
international incident.

The three youths had driven from Berlin to Munich to
visit the tomb of Nazi agitator Horst Wessel. They had
parked the car near the tomb and were looking at the
perpetual flame that burned inside the monument,
when a gang of young German toughs began throwing
rocks at the Americans and their car. The natural reaction of the well-conditioned boys was to fight the German bullies and give them a good drubbing. But Jack,
even though he was as furious as his companions, told
the boys to retreat.

On the trip back to the hotel, young Jack explained
his refusal to fight. According to his reasoning, the
Germans had undoubtedly thought that the three boys
were English—for the car they were driving had English license plates. Moreover, it wouldn't do for the
son of the United States Ambassador to Britain to be
arrested for brawling in the streets with a gang of
German toughs. The significance of the encounter, Jack
glumly pointed out to Macdonald and White, was that
Hitler's rantings were making sense to the German
youths and their hate against the British had been
roused to such an extent that they would gladly follow
the "Fuehrer" in war. It was a prophetic analysis.

Only a week before the war broke out, Jack finished a trip to Egypt and returned to Berlin, where he stayed at the United States embassy.

The embassy's phone had been disconnected and the light bulbs had all been removed. Suddenly U.S. Charge d'Affairs Alex Kirk asked young Kennedy to come where they could be in private, and Kirk spoke in a whisper to Jack, who leaned close to be sure to catch every word.

"John, you must take this message to your father in England," Kirk whispered. "Tell him that the date of the war has already been set. The Nazis will strike within three days of the anniversary of the Battle of Tannenberg, which is August 27. Now leave Germany at once before they detect you."

Jack left Berlin immediately, the secret locked in his memory. He arrived in London, just in time to relay the message to his father. For, as Kirk had warned, the Nazis were ready to declare war. On September 1, 1939, —five days from the anniversary of the Battle of Tannenberg, the Nazis mercilessly invaded Poland.

Twenty-four hours after the Nazis declared war, young Jack found himself personally involved in the tumult. At three o'clock one morning an emergency phone call to Ambassador Kennedy's summer house brought the news that the British ocean liner, *Athenia,* had been torpedoed in the Atlantic Ocean. On board the sinking ship were 1,418 passengers, of whom 300 were American citizens. With his customary speed in times of crisis, the Ambassador awakened Jack and dispatched him to Glasgow to take care of the American survivors who might be rescued and brought to shore.

Of even deeper importance, the Ambassador wanted to find out exactly how the sinking had occurred.

Arriving in Glasgow, Jack fell heir to a ticklish and ugly situation. The Americans who were rescued from the *Athenia* wanted to return home guarded by a convoy of American warships. Almost hysterical after their 12-hour lifeboat vigil at sea, the American passengers were not willing to listen to young Kennedy's explanation that their safest course would be to return on a clearly marked American passenger vessel. America was still a neutral, Jack said, and the presence of American warships could be mistaken by the Germans as a breach of United States neutrality.

One furious passenger yelled: "We've got six billion dollars worth of United States Navy and they won't do this for us?" A hysterical college girl shook her fist at Jack and stated that the passengers would refuse to go home if he didn't get them a convoy immediately.

Amidst all the confusion, Jack managed to piece together the story of what happened at sea: the *Athenia* had been fired upon without warning by a Nazi submarine and many of the passengers had been trapped and drowned. Quickly, he made arrangements to get back to London where he could report to his father. American citizens had been mercilessly killed by the Nazis, Jack mused, as his train sped back to London. It was the first time, he thought. Then he shuddered as a thought crossed his mind—it probably would not be the last time.

Not long after, Jack sailed for home to finish his college studies.

VI

"Why England Slept"

In September of 1939, a few weeks after Germany marched into Poland, Jack Kennedy returned to Harvard for his senior year. The attention of the entire world was centered on the steaming cauldron of war-torn Europe. Jack's tour of the capitals of the Continent as an aide for his father left him with a fresh viewpoint of the European crisis. He soon discovered that he had become somewhat of a celebrity on the Harvard campus. "I am quite a seer around here," he wrote to his father who was still in Europe.

Nor was that all he discovered. His observations of Europe in turmoil gave an immediacy and a fascination to his courses in international politics. Eagerly, he signed up for additional courses in government and in economics. He wrote editorials for the *Crimson*. Carried on by his growing interest, his grades climbed to a "B" average. Most important—he realized again, in a stronger way, that stretching the muscles of a sharp mind could be as much plain fun as flexing the muscles of an athletic body. In short, he was learning; and it was an exhilarating feeling to realize the strength and perception with which his brain could be applied to a problem. For the first time in his life, Jack was doing really well in his studies. Avidly, he plunged further into the intricacies of his scholastic world.

His rising grades enabled him to try for a degree with honors in political science. To qualify for the honors degree Jack had to write a lengthy thesis. His subject—"Appeasement at Munich"—a study of a key foreign policy blunder that had helped drive England and all of Europe into a bloody war.

During his trips through Europe, Jack had been forcibly struck by the criticisms against Neville Chamberlain, the British Prime Minister. It was Chamberlain who in 1938 had met with Hitler in Munich and allowed the Nazis to overrun Czechoslovakia without any opposition. Chamberlain's actions averted immediate war in Europe, but by appeasing Hitler he gave the Germans an even greater strength. This strength, it was clear, would soon turn in full fury against England.

For months, Jack studied the problem; he read old Parliamentary debates, Foreign Office minutes and comments in the English press. Finally, he did his writing.

At first, Jack's thesis was considered to be a typical college student's paper. It used big words and its organization was spotty. But if the thesis was weak in some respects, it had unsuspected strength and impact in other areas. Kennedy was absolutely impartial in describing the crisis taking place in Europe. Like a doctor performing an operation trying to find a cancerous growth hidden deep in the patient's body, Jack probed the situation.

With the same detached air Kennedy launched his own argument. Analytically, he traced the half-hearted British reaction to the rearming of Germany. He pointed out that it was the pacifist groups, the self-interested industrialists, and petty party politics that caused Britain, as a whole, to ignore the impending challenge from across the English Channel. The world, Jack felt, had become too emotionally involved over the issues of Munich to see the problem clearly. Chamberlain didn't yield Munich because he was afraid of the German army. It was the forces behind Chamberlain— the over-all apathy, a concern with profit and security, pacifism—that forced Chamberlain to act the way he did. ". . . The critics (of Chamberlain) have been firing at the wrong target," Jack wrote. "The Munich Pact itself should not be the object of criticism but rather the underlying factors, such as the state of British opinion and the condition of Britain's armaments which made 'surrender' inevitable."

One of the most disturbing points of Jack's thesis was that democratic nations, such as Great Britain and the United States, might not be able to meet the harsh demands of war without becoming totalitarian states themselves. A democratic government, subject to the will of the people, moves slowly. England's current lack of strength lent weight to his argument. By contrast, the fast-moving force of Nazism, which demanded the utmost in immediate action from German industry, was able to build a huge war machine quickly. It was a sobering thought.

Moreover, young Jack saw the challenge that was facing the United States. America must rearm itself as fast as possible, he stated, if we were to save American democracy. America could save itself only through strength, and must not allow itself to fall into the trap of apathy that had almost strangled Britain. Running

72   BOYS' LIFE OF JOHN F. KENNEDY

deep throughout Jack's paper was the theme of citizen-sacrifice. People in a democracy must be willing to help their government in times of crisis—they must think of what they can *do for*, rather than *receive from* the government. Twenty years later Jack would replay this theme in a major chord as he attempted to rally the American people in another time of crisis.

In the early spring of 1940, at the very time Jack Kennedy was turning in his thesis for grading by his Harvard professors, the events in Europe proved the accuracy of many of his arguments. The modern German army, equipped with new tanks and dive bombers, was sweeping through an ill-prepared Europe like a deadly scythe.

Apparently nothing could stand in the way of the Nazi horde. Holland and Belgium collapsed at the very first blows. France, with the Maginot Line—the so-called perfect defense—was next. This vast French network of pill boxes, mounting huge cannons and machine guns and supported by underground tunnels through which whole battalions of soldiers could march at a moment's notice, fell easy prey to the motorized German army. German tanks swept around the end of the French defense system, and French machine guns and cannons, prepared to fight an onrushing foe, were outflanked, outmaneuvered, and helpless. The confidence of Frenchmen in their proud army collapsed. And France surrendered to Germany.

Only England fought on. The British army in Europe fell back against the sea at Dunkirk. Thousands of boats—excursion steamers, ferryboats, sailboats and pleasure yachts—set sail from England's shores to rescue the British soldiers from complete annihilation.

Miraculously the rescue operation was successful and the British army was saved to fight another day.

The fate of Britain was questionable. The danger was so great that at times it seemed as though she, too, might succumb. Only the indomitable British spirit, fanned now to new heights by Winston Churchill, was keeping Britain alive in her time of crisis.

And so, while Jack Kennedy graduated from Harvard with all the tradition, pomp and pageantry that are a part of a Harvard commencement, Europe was in flames. Jack's thesis, describing the political background of the conflagration, was well-received. He graduated *cum laude* in political science with a *magna cum laude* grade for his thesis. "Two things I always knew about you," cabled a proud Ambassador Kennedy to his son. "One that you are smart. Two that you are a swell guy. Love. Dad."

Earlier in the year, elated by the fine reception accorded to his thesis, Jack had decided to try to have it published in book form. Ambassador Kennedy agreed it would be wise and father and son began a lengthy correspondence regarding certain points.

Jack's father felt that in some respects Jack had gone too far in absolving British politicians of the weaknesses of their nation at the time of the Munich Pact. With a great deal of candor, the elder Kennedy said that while Jack could blame the British people as a whole for not caring, he could not absolve the politicians from *all* responsibility. After all, the Ambassador maintained, a politician must do more than just listen to the thoughts of the people. "(The politician) is supposed to look after the national welfare," he wrote to

Jack, "and to attempt to educate the people. . . ." Jack
accepted much of his father's advice as he rewrote the
thesis for book publication.

If some of the guidelines of thought were provided
by the Ambassador, most of them were supplied by
young Jack as he relentlessly drove home his point. "To
say that democracy has been awakened by the events of
the last few weeks is not enough," Jack wrote. "Any
person will awake when the house is burning down.
What we need is an armed guard that will wake up
when the fire first starts or, better yet, one that will not
permit a fire to start at all.

"We should profit by the lesson of England and make
our democracy work. We must make it work right now.
Any system of government will work when everything
is going well. It is the system that functions in the
pinches that survives."

The words were strong, and their thought carried a
measured tread of urgency. The theme was timely and
Jack had firsthand observations to back it up. The message was clear to all who read it. The United States was
approaching war. There could probably be no escaping
the tragedy. But the causes of the war, the softness and
laxity of government, must be understood and guarded
against in the future.

Jack called his book, *Why England Slept*. It was an
immediate success, and made the best-seller list almost
overnight. It was quite a feat for a first book from a
23-year-old author. Ambassador Kennedy sent copies
of it to the Queen of England, Prime Minister Churchill,
and to his son's former economics teacher, Professor
Laski. In a letter to Jack, the Ambassador told his son:
"You would be surprised how a book that really makes
the grade with high-class people stands you in good

stead for years to come. . . . There is no doubt that you have done yourself a great deal of good."

If Jack Kennedy, as his father wrote, was doing himself a great deal of good, the same could not be said of the father about his own career. Ambassador Kennedy, exposed now to the brutal German bombing of London, solidified his stand against America's involvement in the war. "When you get as close to it as I am," he told reporters, "if you could see what the bombs have done to London and to those who have to remain there, you would understand why I say this is not our war."

In message after message sent back to President Roosevelt, Ambassador Kennedy repeated his views. America must abstain from the conflict and must arm itself for self-defense.

Ambassador Kennedy thought that much of Europe would fall under communist rule. In this prediction he proved to be right. As he saw the German blitz smashing London, he also told the President that aid to Britain would be futile. The cause, in his opinion, was lost. It was one of the few times in his life that Joseph P. Kennedy was dead wrong.

Not long after Jack's book appeared, Ambassador Kennedy's views on the English situation were published in a Boston newspaper. In an interview that he thought was "off-the-record," he spoke frankly of his fear for the future of democracy in England. When the story was picked up by newspapers all over the world, Ambassador Kennedy's usefulness as a diplomatic representative was destroyed. There was nothing he could do but resign. And he did.

During this time, Jack's elder brother, Joe, Jr., also wasn't winning any political popularity contests among the powers-that-be. Jack, at 23, was a bestselling author; Joe, Jr., at 25 had become active in national politics and in his first campaign had won a place as a delegate to the Democratic National Convention.

The Democratic convention machinery was prepared to name Roosevelt as its candidate for a precedent-shattering third term. Young Joe was unalterably opposed to such a maneuver, and he was vehement in making his thoughts known on the matter. When the roll was called, the President had 946 votes. He had only needed 551 to gain the nomination. But young Joe didn't vote for Roosevelt. Pledged to give his vote to James A. Farley, who also opposed a third term for Roosevelt, young Joe resisted every effort to get him to change his mind and make the vote for Roosevelt unanimous. Even when other delegates threatened Joe that they would call his father in London and get him to change his vote, Joe wouldn't give in.

When delegates finally did phone the Ambassador to ask if he would try to change young Joe's mind, the Ambassador flatly replied: "No. I wouldn't think of telling him what to do. He thinks he would be going back on his word."

After the convention, Joe, Jr. spoke out along with his father against Roosevelt's foreign policy of aid to England. Joe, Jr., at one point, went so far as to say the United States would be better off if it bartered with a Europe dominated by Nazis than it would be if it engaged in all-out war as a British ally.

The publicly-stated peace-at-all-cost views of Joe Kennedy, Sr. and Joe Kennedy, Jr. were not popular in many quarters. As the future developed, they turned out to be shortsighted views as well, and when this became obvious, father and son quickly admitted it.

But whatever the shortcomings of their position, no one denied that it was honestly felt, honestly arrived at and publicly defended despite its unpopularity.

The rigid keep-out-of-war position espoused by Joe, Sr. and Joe, Jr. seems to have been endorsed only partially by Jack, who had made his point about the *cause* of the problem in *Why England Slept*. Jack, as his mind stretched from the hard thinking he was doing, was able to see both sides of the picture; Joe, Jr. impulsive to a fault, was narrower in his philosophy. Although the two brothers differed somewhat in their political positions, they were the closest of friends, now on somewhat more of an equal footing. Together, they planned their summer at Hyannis Port.

VII

The Calm Before the Storm

THE SUMMER of 1940 was the last time all nine Kennedy children would ever be together. Off just a little way into the future was a dreaded world war that would involve America and the Kennedys in the most personal and intimate way. Nations in Europe were falling one by one to the armies of Germany and Adolf Hitler. In the Far East, Japan was building a huge military machine. It was clear to all who knew international politics, and few families in America knew more of international politics than the Kennedys, that the whole world would soon be plunged into the darkness of the greatest war in human history. Today, England was fighting; eventually America would come to her aid.

But, so far, the years had been extremely kind to the irrepressible tribe of Kennedy children.

Gathered at the family's summer home on the seashore at Hyannis Port, the family presented itself as a group of young men and women with extremely bright futures. Young Joe had already made his mark as a controversial politician. Jack had authored a best-selling book; sister Kathleen was a newspaperwoman working for the *Washington Times-Herald*. The six younger children stood in awe of their illustrious elder brothers and sister, but awe, in the Kennedy household, didn't

78

stand for much as the Kennedys competed with each other in every conceivable manner.

When one of Jack's friends came down for a weekend, he found the big Cape Cod house filled to overflowing with a gay group of the family's school and college friends.

"The next thing I knew," recounted the friend, "all of us were choosing up sides to play touch football, and Kathleen was calling the plays for the team I was on. There was something doing every minute. The conversation at the dinner table was wonderful, lively and entertaining, ranging from the war and Washington politics to books, sports and show business. I don't think America had another family quite like the Kennedys."

The Kennedy children, the boys and the girls, were all athletes. To visitors, the only time the children ever seemed to relax was when they were sleeping, and they rarely seemed to do that. Whenever they gathered together, they were ready to play.

Touch football has always been a favorite pastime of the Kennedys—even in later life, the brothers-in-law and sisters-in-law all had to be good players. Friends remember the time that Bobby Kennedy, intent on running for a touchdown, ran headlong into a barbed wire fence and bounced off it, his face streaming with blood. Scorning first aid, he kept on playing. Many years later, Jack would compliment Bobby's petite new wife, Ethel, by telling a friend, "She's really good—you ought to see her run and pass."

In the summer of 1940, with the world moving irrevocably toward disaster, the Kennedys seemed intent on milking the last months of peace. Instinctively, they

could feel that this was the end of the golden childhood of a fabulous family and, concurrently, the end of
the golden childhood of a fabulous nation. Within
months, both family and nation would pick up the
cudgels of war not as children, but as adults, intent on
their task. Success in war, however, would bring no
return to childhood—it was a complex, harried, cruel
and adult world that waited for the Kennedys and for
America at the end of the rainbow of 1940.

Ferociously, then, they competed at Hyannis Port in
1940—at football, at tennis, at sailing, at anything.
And always, as the Kennedys battled, they grew, collec-
tively and individually. They delivered, one to another,
the strength and confidence they would need in the
forthcoming years. As they girded themselves for the
uncertain future, one could almost feel the underlying
premise behind the Kennedy vigor and vitality: "For
now, it's good to be alive."

Justice William O. Douglas of the United States Supreme Court, described the Kennedys' close-knit life this
way: "Most youngsters, as they grow up, seek their main
stimulation and interests outside the home, but the Kennedys found these things in their own family circle. . . .
It was an exciting home, a good place to be, full of fun
and games and plenty of fascinating talk. It was hard for
them to find anything as fascinating outside. This is why
they are so attached to each other, and so secure."

Later, Joseph E. Dineen, a veteran Boston political
reporter, would say this of the Kennedys: "The sons
and daughters of Joseph P. Kennedy are not interested
in money *per se*. Each is a millionaire; their father saw
to that years ago when he set up trust funds in their
names. They were trained from childhood for public
service, and their avowed and dedicated purpose is to

do the most good with their money while they are here. A Kennedy cannot gauge his success by how much he earns. The only yardstick in the family is: 'What have you accomplished?' "

Too soon, the idyllic summer ended. By the time the next summer came Joe, Jr. had enlisted in the Navy as an aviation cadet.

Jack, who had planned to continue his studies at Yale Law School, changed his mind and went to the west coast to study business at Stanford University for six months. Then, anxious to travel again, he took a long trip through South America. When he returned, war was closing in on America and Jack Kennedy prepared to enlist in the armed forces.

Significantly, where Joe, Jr. had found it easy to get into the Navy, Jack had to scale a major hurdle to join up. But to Jack, characteristically, a hurdle was only something to be conquered.

Originally, he had wanted to enlist in the Air Corps, but he knew that the back injury he'd suffered playing football at Harvard would disqualify him. Then, he hoped to join the Army, but he found himself turned down because Army doctors believed that his back could not stand the strain placed on a combat infantry-man.

For a Kennedy to be unable to meet a challenge because he was physically lacking was a galling experience. So, under the direction of physical training instructors, Jack went through five months of rigorous exercises to strengthen his back. Finally, he won a commission in the Navy.

At first Jack was assigned to an intelligence job which had him tied down to a desk in Washington. But a desk in Washington was not Jack's idea of how to fight a war. He used all his influence—and his father's influence—to win a combat assignment.

Late in 1942, Jack realized his ambition and was assigned to training duty at Patrol Torpedo Boat School. For six months, Jack learned all the intricacies of handling one of these rugged and dangerous craft.

Nothing could have put a tougher test to his ailing back. The flimsy boats—dependent on speed for protection rather than armor plate—drove across the waves at speeds of about 50 miles per hour, jolting, jarring, and jimmying their crews with relentless force.

At PT-Boat School, young Jack presented somewhat of a puzzle to his fellow officers. He was six feet tall, but skinny as a rail, and quickly got the nickname of "Shafty" for his slight build. His brown hair, tumbling over his forehead, gave him an extremely boyish look— younger by far than his 25 years. Several times, out of uniform, Jack was mistaken for an officer's son or perhaps a brand new recruit by men who later learned, much to their chagrin, that young Kennedy was to be their instructor on how to handle PT-Boats.

If Jack had some trouble impressing his fellow Navy men as an old salt on shore, he had none once the boats were at sea. As he neared the end of his training, Jack's superiors graded him as near perfect in ship handling and "very willing and conscientious."

Early in 1943, Jack was shipped out of San Francisco to join the vast sea-air-ground attack against Japan that was taking shape in the South Pacific. Jack was based on the island of Rendova, which is south of New Georgia. Soon, he was made skipper of his own PT-Boat, the *PT-109*, with its crew of two other officers and ten enlisted men.

Part Two
WAR

VIII

"So this is how it feels
to be killed"

PT-109 saw hard service. Her skipper, Lieutenant Junior Grade John F. Kennedy, drove her up and down the waters of the Solomon Islands, sinking Japanese infantry landing barges and strafing shore installations. It was dangerous duty, but Kennedy's adroit handling of the 77-foot boat seemed to make his crew believe their flimsy craft was almost indestructible.

By August of 1943, Kennedy had piloted the *PT-109* through 30 missions as he and his squadron played a part in the American counterthrust against the Japanese forces entrenched around the South Pacific island of New Georgia. The boat had seen fierce combat, often skating the thin line dividing danger from death, but Kennedy, his crew, and the *PT-109* had remained unharmed.

The thirty-first mission was different.

Kennedy's fight for life started on August 2, 1943, when the boat was on patrol about 40 miles away from its home base. It was 2 A.M.—a dark and squally night. Ships of the Japanese fleet were busy taking Japanese

85

troops from the island beaches and transferring them
northward to other islands from where they might fight
again. Somewhere above were Japanese float planes,
assigned to the task of following the wake of American
torpedo boats, and blowing them sky high with bomb
attacks.

Kennedy was at the wheel of the boat, on the little
open bridge near the bow. To keep the boat's movement silent, the middle engine of PT-109 was running
at low speed; the other two engines were idling in neutral. All hands were at their battle stations, straining
their eyes looking for enemy targets hidden by the inky
blackness of the night.

Close at hand, though Skipper Kennedy and his men
didn't realize it, was the destroyer *Amagiri* of the Japanese Imperial Navy. On the destroyer's bridge, Captain
Kohei Hanami also peered through the night. His ship
had been bedeviled all day by American planes and
now he was worried about the ever-present American
PT-Boats. Suddenly Hanami saw a PT-Boat moving
slowly less than half a mile away.

"Starboard ten degrees!" Hanami yelled to his helms-
man and the destroyer bore off slightly to the right.

On the PT-Boat, Skipper Kennedy and his crew
cursed the black night that hid the enemy from them.
Suddenly a lookout called, "Ship at two o'clock!" Kennedy, startled, saw the fast grim-looking Japanese destroyer bearing down on him.

"Hey," Kennedy yelled, "look at this!" he hit the
general alarm button and shouted "Sound general quarters!"

At the same moment Kennedy signaled the engineer
to throttle the two idling engines full ahead. On the
bow, Ensign George Ross, who had been scanning

ahead with a pair of nighttime binoculars, feverishly
tried to load a shell into the 37-mm. cannon the crew
had installed there in makeshift fashion on a big log.
Ross managed to get the shell in the gun but never had
a chance to close the cannon's breech.

At 30 knots, the destroyer smashed into the plywood
PT-Boat, cut the smaller craft cleanly in two, and
rushed on without slowing. *PT-109* broke apart with an
unearthly wrenching sound, and burst into flames.

Kennedy and his radioman, John Maguire, were
slammed to the deck of their boat with terrific force,
and Maguire could hear Jack gasping from the pain of
the impact.

The destroyer pulled ahead, and continued to drive
on into the black night. Captain Hanami ordered his
gun crews to fire a few rounds at the wreckage, but
they gave it up when they saw that the boat was already ablaze from the high-octane gasoline that the PT
engines used. The PT-Boat's destruction was complete.
There could be no survivors, they thought. And, even
as young Jack was thrown to the deck, he thought, "So
this is how it feels to be killed."

But there were survivors. Fortunately, Kennedy's
half of the PT-Boat didn't sink immediately. When he
regained his breath, Kennedy began counting survivors
and found that four crew members were clinging to the
wreckage. Shouting to find out if there were any more,
Jack heard answering hails from six more men who
were in the water nearby. One of the men, the engineer
Pat McMahon, had surfaced in the middle of the flames
and his face, hands and arms were burned black. Another survivor, gunner's mate Charles Harris, was close
to McMahon and tried to help him. But Harris had

injured one of his legs in the crash and couldn't kick
hard enough to swim properly.

Harris yelled for Kennedy. "Skipper! Skipper!" he
kept calling, "McMahon's burned bad. Can you give
him a hand?"

Kennedy quickly dived into the water and reached
the two men in a couple of minutes. Grabbing Mc-
Mahon, Kennedy towed him back to the still-floating
portion of the PT-Boat where the other survivors pulled
the injured man aboard. Then Kennedy swam back to
pick up Harris.

Reaching Harris again, Kennedy held him afloat
while he took off the injured man's heavy sweater and
shoes. Then he helped him put his life jacket back on
and started to help him back to the wreckage.

But Harris' injured leg began stiffening and he
couldn't swim.

"Skipper," he said, "I can't swim. I can't make it."

"Try," replied Kennedy.

"I can't go any farther," Harris protested.

Kennedy looked at Harris and said: "For a man from
Boston, you're really putting on some exhibition out
here, Harris."

Harris tried, and Kennedy helped him along. But it
took the two men an hour to reach the hulk, for it kept
drifting away with the current and wind.

The forward half of the *PT-109* had watertight com-
partments which kept it afloat, and the 11 survivors
sprawled on the wreckage, dazed and frightened. Mc-
Mahon began to suffer from his burns and Bill John-
ston, another engineer, was retching from having swallowed a lot of gasoline.

The situation was desperate. The men had no food,

no water, and worst of all, no medical supplies. The skies to the north were aflame with the fires of war, but on their black stretch of sea, there appeared to be no hope of a fast rescue.

Slowly, the night wore itself away. When the first gray light of the false dawn brought no sign of help, the stunning realization came that they must have been written off as missing in action.

The boat began listing and settling deeper in the water. To the northeast, south and west were islands swarming with tough, jungle-trained Japanese troops who would show the Americans no mercy.

What could they do next? The question was uppermost in Kennedy's mind. The responsibility for saving his crewmates pressed heavily on him.

"What do you want to do if the Japs come out?" Kennedy asked his shipmates. "Surrender or fight?"

"Fight with what?" asked one of the men.

It was a tough question.

The crew had only been able to salvage a single Thompson submachine gun, six 45-caliber automatics, and one 38.-caliber pistol. Not much defense if they should have to fight.

"Well, what do you want to do?" Kennedy asked again.

"Anything you say, Mr. Kennedy," someone said. "You're the boss."

Kennedy thought for a couple of minutes and then asked again for the opinions of the crewmen. But discussion led to an argument, and Kennedy realized that he would have to make whatever decisions were necessary.

The wreckage on which they were sprawled was sinking faster now, and he ordered everyone but the wounded men into the water. Then the hulk turned upside down, and Kennedy reasoned that it would be best to abandon it and swim to a small island about three miles away to the southeast.

The men by now were within a mile of a large island held by the Japanese and they could see a Japanese army camp filled with trucks and men. So when Kennedy declared they were drifting toward the island, the men abandoned their sanctuary without second thought.

Kennedy was very matter-of-fact about making the decision that they would have to swim for their lives.

"We're going to the small island," he said quietly. "We'll have to swim for it. Everyone hang onto the log. I'll take care of McMahon."

When everyone had started out, Kennedy took two long straps hanging from McMahon's kapok life jacket, put them in his teeth, and started swimming, towing McMahon behind him.

An hour passed. Kennedy was swimming ahead of the other men who were holding onto the huge timber that had been used to mount the 37-mm. cannon on the deck. Every so often, the skipper would stop to get his breath and cough from the water he'd swallowed. Then he'd start again, and stop, and start again, and rest again saying, "How are you, Mac?"

With torturous slowness the group edged towards the island. Finally, after five hours of steady swimming, they reached shore. Kennedy helped McMahon over the coral reefs which cut them both badly. Then the young skipper and the wounded man he'd rescued collapsed on the sand. In total, young Kennedy had been in the water for almost 15 straight hours.

The survivors of *PT-109* crawled onto the wind-swept atoll and lay exhausted among the palm trees. But Jack didn't rest for long. Dusk was falling and Kennedy wanted to swim out into the channel and try to signal a PT-Boat, should one happen to pass by in the night while on patrol.

Kennedy explained to his crew that the boats of their own squadron would be using Ferguson Passage—only a few miles beyond the next little island—and he planned to swim to the middle of the passage, tread water, and signal for help.

Without saying anything more, Jack picked up the ship's lantern, put on a life jacket, tied the 38 pistol around his neck, and began shuffling toward the water.

In the twilight, he swam toward the reef. Suddenly, he saw a big fish pass just a few yards away.

What thoughts must have flashed through Kennedy's tired mind? How much self-control could a man have when he had heard stories about these vicious fish—torpedo-shaped barracudas—that were supposed to swim up under a man and bite his legs off?

Nevertheless, he continued his lonely swim. Finally, he made it into Ferguson Passage. There, chilled and numb, he tread water and cradled the lantern hoping that rescue might come.

But no boat came through the channel. Discouraged and at the very limit of his endurance, Kennedy started back toward shore, only to find the current was against him and getting stronger. He seemed to stop caring, his mind began to wander, and he drifted with the current in an almost unconscious state, afloat thanks only to his life jacket, but still he held onto the heavy lantern which was his only link with other living men.

Back on shore, Kennedy's men worried about their skipper. They knew the perils he was facing in the channel and none wanted to talk about them. But they kept their hope up for him.

The men took turns watching for his return. Kennedy's plan had been that if he found a boat he would signal "Roger" on the lantern. The men would flash "Wilco" back to him.

But when Kennedy found himself drifting past the island with the current, he flashed the light once to his men and yelled "Roger," and the men went out on the reef in a vain attempt to catch him as he was swept helplessly by.

The current pushed Kennedy in long sweeping circles all through the night, moving him like driftwood past the Japanese-held islands to the north and east. And like a playful child, the current finally let Kennedy out of its clutches the next morning—in almost exactly the same spot in Ferguson Passage where it had captured him 12 hours earlier.

Once again Kennedy started toward land. Making it to the reef, he picked his way along the jagged coral, slashing his bare feet on the sharp and poisonous rocks. Finally, he made his way to the island and crawled up the beach on his hands and knees, vomiting from exhaustion and from the salt water he had swallowed during the night. As his men gathered around him, Kennedy looked up at his third officer, Ensign George Ross, and said, "Okay, you try it tonight." Then he passed out.

Back at Kennedy's base, the squadron had given up all hope for the 13 men on *PT-109*. Actually the *109* hadn't been scheduled to go on patrol when it had. But a Japanese air attack on the base that afternoon had put some other boats of the squadron out of commission, and Kennedy and his crew, who had been slated for a day off, suddenly had to return to duty.

In a solemn moment, the men at the base gathered and held a memorial service for the men of *PT-109* who supposedly had been lost in action. One officer wrote a letter to the mother of one of Kennedy's crewmates to tell her that her son had died for a cause which he believed to be "stronger than any of us." The letter went on to say that young Jack Kennedy, the son of the former Ambassador to Great Britain, had also lost his life in the same action.

IX

Help from the Natives

THAT EVENING Ensign Ross swam out to Ferguson Passage to wait for a passing PT-Boat as his skipper had done the night before. But his luck was as bad as Kennedy's.

On shore the men were beginning to suffer terribly from thirst. There was no fresh water on the island, not even coconuts to crack open for their sweet-tasting milk. Kennedy lay awake most of the night, sick and cold and worried about the future.

In the morning, when Ross returned, Kennedy decided to move the men to an island closer to Ferguson Passage where they would have a better chance of being rescued. The spot he had in mind was somewhat bigger and had more trees. Once again the small tired band set off. Kennedy was in the lead towing McMahon by the straps of the kapok life jacket as he had done the previous day. The other men gathered around the big log and again began to swim.

McMahon was still alive. His burns were beginning to fester and had the angry look that accompanies infection.

Kennedy, too, by this time, was in bad shape. He swam ahead slowly and painfully, like a man in a slow-

94

motion film. His feet were blistered and horribly swollen from the coral cuts, and he had to stop swimming from time to time to throw up, this from the nauseous effect of the salt water he was swallowing.

Three hours later the haggard crew finally reached their new island and as they crawled ashore, were greeted by the sight of ripe coconuts lying on the sand. Quickly they broke the fruit open and gulped the delicious milk. Just as quickly their stomachs, which had been without food for three days, rebelled at the rich coconut milk, giving the men violent stomach cramps. Some of the men were so hungry they even tried eating raw snails, but they tasted so terrible the experiment quickly ended.

That night, rain fell in torrents and the men, frantic for fresh water, went around to all the tree trunks and leaves to lick up the falling water. But next morning, they found out why the rain water, which should have tasted sweet, had tasted so bitter. The island had been used as a roosting place for birds and all the bushes were covered with droppings. Wryly, the men named the spot Bird Island.

That morning was the fourth day the men had been shipwrecked. Hope for their rescue was fading and one of the men, spying the rosary that another crewman wore, said: "Maguire, give that necklace a working over."

Maguire trailed the rosary beads through his fingers. "Yes," he said, "don't worry. I'll take care of all you fellows."

Still there were no signs of American boats or planes. A Japanese barge slowly circled the atoll but didn't see the Americans lying in the underbrush. Japanese planes flew by in a constant stream, and the men stayed covered so the Japanese fliers couldn't spot them.

Kennedy was thinking ahead. He kept looking at another island, named Nauru, which lay next to the passage and he decided to try to swim there next. Their only hope was to establish a base as close as possible to Ferguson Passage and from there flag down an American boat.

Picking Ensign Ross to accompany him, Kennedy started out to swim the half mile to Nauru Island. Inching along, their muscles protesting every bit of the way, it took the two men more than an hour to reach their destination. Again beach coral cut deeply into Ross' and Kennedy's feet as they half-walked and half-crawled across the island. At any moment they expected to find a patrol of Japanese soldiers.

What thoughts ran through their minds? Both men were starving and they could either die of malnutrition or be shot from ambush by the Japanese. Each step was torture.

But instead of finding the island occupied by Japanese troops, Ross and Kennedy discovered only the deserted wreck of an enemy landing barge. Investigating the hulk, they found a cask of water and some ancient hardtack biscuits. The two feasted on the first real food they'd had since *PT-109* had gone down.

Again the two men stayed up all night, waiting by the water's edge for American boats to pass in the night. Again there were no boats.

The next morning, Kennedy prowled around the island and discovered a one-man dugout canoe that some natives had hidden under palm trees. Elated by the discovery, he paddled out into the passage that night but, once more, could find no rescue boats.

With such bad luck facing him, Kennedy paddled back alone to the island where the other men lay hidden, taking with him the welcome present of the water keg and a supply of hardtack biscuits.

But going back to Nauru, Kennedy was in for more bad times. Suddenly, his tiny craft was swamped by a quick tropical storm, leaving him alone in the center of the rain squall. Fortunately, a party of friendly natives, passing by in their war canoe, spotted the young skipper struggling in the water, picked him up, and took him to Nauru. Ross, in hiding on the island, thought Kennedy looked like a goner when he saw the primitive natives, with sharp bones piercing their nostrils, finally bring Jack ashore.

For a long time Kennedy and Ross tried to talk with the natives in pidgin English, the universal language of the South Pacific, but it was no use; the natives didn't understand. "Rendova, Rendova, Rendova," the two Americans kept on saying. "Americans, Americans, Americans."

Finally Kennedy picked up a smooth coconut husk and scratched a message on its shell with a penknife:

ELEVEN ALIVE NATIVE KNOWS POSITION
AND REEFS NAURU ISLAND KENNEDY

Then, handing the shell to one of the natives, Kennedy again said, "Rendova, Rendova, Rendova"—the name of the base where the other PT-Boats in the squadron were stationed.

One of the natives finally understood and told the others in his party what Kennedy wanted. Before they

left, the natives showed the two Americans where
they could find a two-man canoe. Then, after a lot of
conversation among themselves, the natives climbed
into their own war canoe and started off in the direction
of Rendova. Watching the natives go, Kennedy and
Ross sat down and passed out.

Kennedy and Ross lay exhausted all day on the
beach, but as evening approached, Kennedy decided
they must try once more to contact the Navy.

Clambering to where the natives had shown them the
two-man dugout canoe, the pair set off into Ferguson
Passage when evening fell. Suddenly the wind changed
and the two found themselves in the middle of a howl-
ing squall. The waves swept down on their tiny craft
and it was swamped. For the third time Kennedy was
in the ocean, swimming for his life.

For two hours the two men struggled against a dangerous tidal current that was trying to sweep them out
to sea. Their goal again was to get back to Nauru.

"Sorry I got you out here, Barney!" shouted Kennedy
over the roar of the wind.

"This would be a great time to say I told you so,"
yelled Ross, "but I won't."

The pair kept swimming and finally they heard the
surf pounding on the reef. Kennedy felt a huge wave
break his grip on the canoe and twist him down and
around in its dangerous currents. Nothing could be
more deadly, and Kennedy expected at any moment to
feel himself slammed with murderous force against the
coral reef with its knife-sharp rocks. Miraculously, he
landed in a little eddy with the ocean swirling gently
around him. Ross, however, was not so fortunate. The

same wave that had delivered Kennedy safe had pounded Ross, and he had deep cuts on his arm and shoulder.

Making their way up the beach, Kennedy had to take the canoe paddles and lay them down one after the other so Ross could walk up the coral on his lacerated feet. Then, again, they collapsed from exhaustion and slept.

As the two men rested, their painful ordeal was drawing to an end. When they woke up the next morning, four natives were standing over them.

One of the natives, speaking in beautiful English, looked at Kennedy and said: "I have a letter for you, sir."

Kennedy tore open the letter and read:

> *On His Majesty's Service. To the Senior Officer, Nauru Island.*
>
> *I have just learned of your presence on Nauru Island. I am in command of a New Zealand infantry patrol operating on New Georgia. I strongly advise that you come with these natives to me. Meanwhile, I shall be in radio communication with your authorities at Rendova, and we can finalize plans to collect the balance of your party. Lieutenant Wincote.*

The rescue couldn't have come at a more opportune moment. Ross' arm had swollen to the size of his thigh from coral poisoning; MacMahon's burns had become badly infected. They would need medical attention within hours.

Kennedy clambered into the natives' canoe. He lay down in the bottom of the tiny craft, and the natives made sure that Japanese planes couldn't see Kennedy by covering him with palm fronds. They started out on the long trip to reach the New Zealand patrol on New Georgia.

That night, Kennedy finally contacted an American PT-Boat at a special rendezvous point. Hearing four shots ring out across the water he fired four shots in answer. Suddenly a PT-Boat swung alongside the canoe and friends pulled Jack aboard.

A few hours later, with the natives guiding the PT-Boat through the shoals and channels, Kennedy arrived at Bird Island to pick up the rest of his crew. Then they set out for home.

On the return trip, one of Kennedy's crewmen drank some medicinal brandy and went to sit on the bow of the PT-Boat with two of the missionary-trained natives who had helped in the rescue. Jack Kennedy, exhausted but happy, watched from the side as the three men sat, their arms around one another, singing a hymn they had learned as children growing up more than ten thousand miles apart:

"Jesus loves me, this I know,
For the Bible tells me so;
Little ones to Him belong,
They are weak, but He is strong.
Yes, Jesus loves me; yes, Jesus love me. . . ."

Just about the time Kennedy was being rescued, his family received a grim telegram that said:

THE SECRETARY OF THE NAVY REGRETS TO INFORM YOU THAT LIEUTENANT J/G JOHN FITZGERALD KENNEDY IS REPORTED MISSING IN ACTION.

Kennedy's return to Rendova was marked by a wild celebration. The stories the survivors told about Kennedy's continued efforts to get help spread quickly through the base. In short order, Kennedy received the Purple Heart and the Navy and Marine Corps Medal. Admiral William F. Halsey signed the citation, which said, in part:

> . . . . *His courage, endurance and excellent leadership contributed to the saving of several lives and was in keeping with the highest traditions of the United States Naval Service . . .*

The rest of the war was an agonizing time for Kennedy. Rather than accept transfer back to the United States when his first tour of duty had been completed, Kennedy volunteered to remain for a second tour in the South Pacific. But he contracted malaria, and his weight, which was always low, dropped alarmingly to 125 pounds. He was now almost 40 pounds underweight, and his Navy friends, who used to call him "Shafty," looked at him with shock. The malaria left him looking terribly sick—as if suffering from malnutrition. Worst of all, his back, which had been injured in the collision with the destroyer, became steadily more painful.

Finally, late in 1943, when Kennedy's squadron was rotated home, an emaciated John F. Kennedy agreed to go into the hospital near Hyannis Port for treatment of his injuries. Navy doctors performed a delicate operation on his spine in an attempt to repair a ruptured disc in his back. The surgery was only partially success-ful and it was a dispirited and dejected combat veteran named Kennedy who spent the long months of recuperation in the hospital.

His spirits, tragically, were to fall even lower before he was to get out of the hospital.

X

The Death of Joe

JACK spent the early months of 1944 in the Chelsea Naval hospital. Then, in August, came news that Joe, Jr. had died in action in the skies over Europe. This time the telegram the Kennedy family received read "killed in action." There was a dread finality to the message and the family was plunged into deep gloom.

When, in 1940, young Joe had echoed the thoughts of his father, that America should not become entangled in the war, he, of course, didn't realize how empty these hopes would become. But, believing in preparation should war come, Joe had enlisted in the Navy, and won his bars and his wings soon after the Japanese bombed Pearl Harbor on December 7, 1941, and brought the United States into the war. Two years later, Joe, Jr. was already rated as one of the top Liberator bomber pilots assigned to patrolling U-Boat Alley in the Atlantic. Day after day, he flew combat missions over the Bay of Biscay, off the coast of France, searching out deadly enemy submarines.

Joe completed one tour of duty, and, as Jack had done in the Pacific, volunteered for a second. When his second tour ended, he was preparing to return home when he heard about a top secret project that would require the skills of an expert pilot. Once again, Joe volunteered.

The secret operation—called "Project Anvil"—was designed to end Germany's latest menace to the British people. It was 1944, and the war was drawing to an end in Europe. Hitler's armies, falling back before the Allied landings in Normandy, unleashed a deadly new weapon—the V-2 rocket.

There was no defense against the new German terror, for the V-2 flew too high and too fast for any interception. The rockets dropped on England without warning, blowing whole blocks of houses into dust. As long as the rockets could fly, there could be no sleep for Britain.

The only hope was to destroy the source from which the rockets came. But this was not easy. The V-2's were launched from huge concrete redoubts in Normandy which were so strong that the usual bombing raids by Flying Fortresses could barely scratch them.

Project Anvil was the code name for a new Allied weapon, a modern plane guided by remote control. The project had been undertaken jointly by the Army and Navy, and had produced a bomber that could be directed to its target by a "mother" plane with as much accuracy as if a human pilot were at the controls.

The robot required a pilot and copilot to get it off the ground with its ten-ton load of high explosives. Once the plane was airborne, the pilot and copilot were supposed to parachute to safety while the "mother" plane flew the robot toward the target. The final step would see the "mother" plane sending the robot plane and its 20,000 pounds of explosives into a controlled dive, so that it would crash and explode directly on the German V-2 launching site.

Joe had volunteered to be the pilot of the robot plane.

The flight started successfully. The robot and its two accompanying "mother" planes took off and headed toward the French coast. What happened after that has never, and will never, be explained. For just before Joe, Jr. and his copilot were to parachute safely to the ground, the explosive-laden plane they were flying blew up in two quick blasts and disintegrated in midair, killing the two men.

Joe was posthumously awarded a garland of decorations—the Navy Cross, the American Defense Medal, and the European-African-Eastern Area Campaign medal. Later, the Navy named a destroyer after young Joe, calling it *U.S.S. Joseph P. Kennedy, Jr.*

Jack Kennedy learned of Joe's death while he was in the hospital.

The death of his older brother jarred him to the very fiber of his soul. It was Joe he had loved, admired, competed with and fought with as a child. It was the pugnacious Joe who set the style and the pace for Jack, and it was in Joe's personality that Jack had found both things to emulate and to reject. Joe had indeed been the anvil upon which the soul of Jack had been forged. They were as close as brothers could be, and yet they were different and competitive. Joe was garrulous, cock-sure, trigger-tempered and immensely charming in his ways. Jack was quiet, reflective and cool—a young man who thought before he acted and who now must continue his thinking and his growing without the presence of the brother he had admired. Joe was dead. Jack would have to carry on alone.

Later, Jack would memorialize his brother in a book privately published in a limited edition called *As We Remember Joe*. In it he would write: "I think that if

the Kennedy children amount to anything now, or
ever amount to anything, it will be due more to Joe's
behavior and his constant example than to any other
factor." It is a beautiful and moving book, a tribute to a
family leader from his brother and from the family he
led.

The next Kennedy to feel the lash of war was 23-
year-old Kathleen. An extremely pretty girl, Kathleen
was still working as a reporter in Washington when she
decided to join the Red Cross. Because of her previous
knowledge of England, she was sent to London. There
she began dating William John Robert Cavendish,
the Marquess of Hartington.

Later Kathleen left her Red Cross job to help her
future husband run for the House of Commons. When
he lost, she was by his side, and, a few months later,
they were married.

Once again the sad fate of war hovered over the
Kennedys. Kathleen and William were able to live together for only a little more than a month in their
London flat. Then William, who was a member of
the famous Coldstream Guards, joined his regiment
and sailed for France and active duty. Kathleen returned to America where she was going to stay with
her family for the duration of the war. But on the tenth
of that September, only three weeks after the family
received notice of young Joe's death during the ill-
fated Project Anvil, the British War Office sent word
that William had been killed in action. He had been
leading an infantry patrol, scouting the terrain in front
of a column of tanks, when he met his death.

In a tragic sequel, four years later, Kathleen perished

when the small chartered plane in which she was flying crashed in southern France.

For Jack, the death of Kathleen's husband further compounded the misery he felt over the death of Joe. The Kennedys, like many other American families, had suffered grievously from the war. As it now drew to a close Joe was dead, Kathleen's new husband was dead, and Jack, after his own brush with death, was in a military hospital still recovering from a painful war injury.

Slowly he gained strength. He was still ill, and still wearing a light brace for his constantly paining back, when, in 1945, he appeared before a Navy board of officers. In a quiet ceremony, a gaunt young war hero retired from active duty, scarred in body and in mind from the most terrible of all wars mankind has known.

Part Three
PEACE AND POLITICS

XI

Politics

THE WAR was ending. In early 1945, a frantic German army was retreating on two fronts. The Japanese were being driven away from one island after another in the South Pacific and their vaunted war machine was crumbling. Slowly, cautiously, a war-torn world looked toward the future and toward peace.

So, too, did Jack Kennedy.

What would he do next? The question weighed heavily on him. Jack was 28, good-looking, a proven war hero and a millionaire. On the debit side of the ledger was the problem of a constantly painful back that still needed a light brace for support. Further, he had no job and no profession. The problem might not have bothered many people in similar circumstances —after all, a millionaire doesn't have to work.

But a playboy's life was not what Jack Kennedy had in mind. The Kennedys, like some other American families of great wealth such as the Roosevelts, the Rockefellers and the Harrimans, did not believe that "play" in itself could ever be a whole way of life. Rather, the Kennedys felt, hard play was only fun when it served as a counterpoint to hard work. As he looked toward the

future, Jack looked for a spot where he could work hard
and perform a useful function.

His decision was a natural one. His greatest talent
had been the ability to use words well and he decided
to put this talent to the test. Journeying to New York, he
applied for a position as a reporter with the Hearst-
owned International News Service and won the job.

His first assignment took him to San Francisco to
cover the initial meeting of a world organization dedicated to peace—the United Nations. The world looked
toward San Francisco with hopeful eyes. The safety
of mankind was at stake. War-torn nations prayed that
the men meeting in America could solve the problems
facing them and set up a structure that would guarantee
that there would never again be another war. Young
Kennedy's copy coming back to INS in New York was
on the pessimistic side, however. With a clear head,
he reasoned that the success of the organization would
depend on the solidarity of the Big Three powers—
America, Great Britain and France. And if these powers
stood firm, there would still be a hard battle with the
onrushing forces of communism.

Jack also made a brief swing through Europe and reported on the British elections and other postwar hap-
penings for INS. There was ferment on the Continent as
the European democracies strove to rebuild their war-
shattered economies. It was an exciting period for a
young man as familiar with international politics as
Jack was—the spirit in Europe was vastly different from
the complacency he had recorded in his early best-
seller *Why England Slept*.

But as Kennedy spent his time tracking down leads
and trying to find and report the meanings behind
veiled diplomatic communiques, he realized that the

life of a reporter was not for him. A reporter, he saw, was once-removed from the real action of the world. A reporter wrote and commented on things that other people did. "It's too passive," he confided to his friends when he talked about the faults of his new career. His strength was returning and he had an urge to move on to more active fields where he might create the news that others would write about.

These were the thoughts in Jack Kennedy's mind when he returned from Europe in 1945 and resigned his position as a reporter for the International News Service.

Legend has it that John F. Kennedy decided to enter politics one evening after a long conversation with his father. Joe, Sr. was supposed to have told Jack that since Joe, Jr. had given his life for his country during the war, it was now up to Jack to uphold the family's tradition of political public service. The entire family would support Jack, his father said. And, as the story goes, Jack heeded his father's urging, and decided to enter politics on the spot.

But the truth is somewhat different. Certainly there was a political tradition in the Kennedy family. To be sure, Joe, Sr. wanted to see this tradition carried on, and certainly he felt it should be carried on by Jack once Joe had died. But this is all too simple—for it takes everything into account except the one most important thing—the remarkable personality of Jack Kennedy.

He had studied politics and government and had written on the subject with an authority rare for so young a man. As his father's helper in England he had actually seen some diplomatic duty. He was a voracious reader and his taste ran toward books about history, government and politics. True, he was a reflective and retiring personality; but underneath his reserve he was a man of action and icy determination. The thought that one day he could be in the top circles of government definitely appealed to him. Deep down, he realized, he was cut out for a political life.

However, there were problems. Jack realized that he was not an outgoing person, and that he would have difficulties slipping into the political framework. He didn't feel at home with strangers, and the minor intrigues of local politics were distasteful to him. He didn't like the backslapping world where the men running for office were adept at shaking hands with two people while talking to a third at the same time. He didn't like to make promises and then break them; that wasn't his way. The creation of a successful political career would, no doubt, have been a much easier task for his gregarious brother Joe.

But this is what he was, he mused, and he was faced now by a choice he really didn't want to make. It could lead to difficulties no matter which way he turned. However, after deep thought, he announced what he would do, and he surprised Boston with his audacious plans. There was a vacant Congressional seat and Jack Kennedy, with no practical political experience behind him was going to run for Congress!

His decision startled Boston's professional politicians. They were hard-bitten men, long used to having things their own way. The past had proved many of their practices corrupt. Some of the politicians, taking their first look at the little David come to challenge them, laughed and decided they would never have to worry about Jack as a threat. Not only was he young, they thought, but he was definitely emaciated from his wartime sicknesses and his skin had the odd yellow cast that one gets from taking Atabrine pills, the drug used to counteract malaria. Jack was the complete opposite of what a Boston politician should be. He didn't wear a derby, he didn't hang around bars, he didn't look like the type who would pad the local patronage rolls with his friends and relatives—and they didn't need it, anyway. In short, the Boston politicians thought that Jack was a fish out of water.

But Jack had his own plans. The first political fight of his career would be his own fight. No one could win it for him. And no matter how much he disliked the idea of becoming a street-corner politician, shaking hands and asking perfect strangers for their vote, he was going to do the job by himself, and do it right.

Jack also had some strong cards that the politicians seemed to overlook. He had the Kennedy name, which should be able to win the votes of the old Irish families who had voted for his grandfather years before. And in politics, where money to finance a strong local campaign can often spell the difference between winning and losing, Jack had another ace up his sleeve in his personal wealth and in the wealth of his family. He could afford the luxury of a well-financed campaign. Best of all, if Jack appeared shy to those he first met, he also had the will to win, and the absolute determination that if he were going to go into politics, he would do it with the same resolution that saved the lives of the men aboard *PT-109*.

116 BOYS' LIFE OF JOHN F. KENNEDY

Boston politicians didn't know the strength of young Jack's character, and this ignorance led them to make a gross miscalculation. The 11th Congressional District, where Jack was running, should prove to be too tough a nut for a newcomer to crack, reasoned the old-time politicos. Sure, it included Harvard University, where Jack had gone to college, but that shouldn't get Jack too many votes. Furthermore, the 11th was one of the roughest and toughest districts in Boston. Its slum areas were among the worst in the nation and its crime rate was one of the highest. No Harvard pipsqueak is going to take these areas away from us, the politicians concluded.

But, the district also had a couple of areas that could help Jack. It covered East Boston, where Jack's father had been born; it also embraced Boston's North End, the home of Jack's mother. The two areas could be mined successfully for voters who remembered the old Kennedy family and their honest brand of politics—a brand quite different from recent scandal-ridden administrations.

Because Jack did not know the area well—as an adult he'd never lived in Boston and his only real contact with the city was during his years at Harvard—he decided to start his own campaign early. Long before any of the other candidates for the job started, Jack was out on his own, ringing doorbells, badgering voters, casing the neighborhood, and organizing a bright young staff.

At the outset, Jack found that filling the shoes of brother Joe wasn't easy. He had few of the qualities that had made Joe such a natural politician. Joe could walk up to a group of truck drivers and make himself at home. Jack found this difficult to do. But, little by little, he overcame his natural shyness and learned to cope with such situations.

Jack's father knew the inner battle his son was going through and the difficulties he was facing. And one day, when Joe, Sr. watched Jack standing on a street corner, shaking hands with strangers, chatting with them, selling his platform to them, and winning their promise to vote for him, he remarked, "I never thought Jack had it in him."

There were times when even Jack thought he might not have the magic touch. Sometimes he'd explain to friends that "if Joe were alive, I wouldn't be doing this." But no one could deny that every day, with each sortie after votes, Jack was gaining confidence in himself. He began to feel a strength in his ability to talk with people, and the maverick group of close supporters he rallied around began to take on a cohesive unity.

Jack's younger brother, Bobby, took over some of the wards where the magic of the Kennedy name could get out the vote. Jack's former roommate, LeMoyne Billings, also came to Boston to help. Timothy (Ted) Reardon, who was an old friend of brother Joe's and was destined to stay with Kennedy in later years, also signed up. And they were joined by a score of other tough, level-headed young men who wanted to clean up Boston politics. The campaign was underway and Jack was picking up a head of steam.

The primary race in which Jack was running was wide open. Because the Republicans were so weak in the district, the Democratic primary winner was a sure thing for Congress. So, all the stops were out and all who wanted to run on the Democratic ticket were plumping hard. All told, nine other people besides Jack were scrambling for the primary victory.

Because Jack had started his campaign earlier than anyone else, the other candidates in the race made light of Jack's efforts. But when they found they couldn't laugh off Jack's growing popularity, they began slinging mud. One candidate called Jack a "poor little rich kid." Another offered to buy him off by promising to make him his secretary in Washington if Jack would stop campaigning. But Jack refused to be bought out or scared by the brickbats his opponents were tossing at him. And when his opponents started the rumor that Jack's father was trying to buy the election, Jack fought back, working harder than before and contacting more voters than ever.

By now, Jack's opponents were beginning to worry. It was well that they should become upset. Jack was touring the district day and night, walking into grocery stores, bars, beauty shops, factories, any place that might hold potential voters. And, as his efforts increased, Jack began looking more and more haggard. People had thought he looked emaciated when he started the campaign and now he was even more gaunt. His back was bothering him badly; he still wore a light brace for additional support and there were times when the strain almost became too much. But Jack kept driving himself, amazing his staff with his endurance and will to win.

Within a few months, Kennedy had become a seasoned campaigner. His careful analysis of the wants of the individual voter, plus his own beliefs, helped him to outline a strong and wise platform. Jack was the only veteran in the race, and he stuck to bread-and-butter issues that he knew would mean a lot to the voters— better housing, benefits for veterans, jobs.

He learned quickly the knack of making people feel

at ease when he met them for the first time. Best of all, his speaking manner improved noticeably and he became more assured when he stood before a hostile audience that might heckle him. But while his words were effective, Jack and his brain-trust began figuring new ways to get votes.

The strategy Jack thought up wasn't brand new. He started giving house parties where a couple of dozen people would gather in the evening for coffee and cake and Jack could come in and talk to them in an informal fashion. But the number of these little parties his staff and family organized was staggering, and Jack attended five or six almost every evening. Jack would saunter in, greet everybody present and settle down in an armchair to talk about the political problems of the moment. His warmth and charm would relax everyone in the room and his boyish looks would soon be forgotten with the force of his words. It was an ideal way for a candidate to meet people and make sure that they'd continue to talk about him to their friends the next day.

Soon, Kennedy's campaign had caught fire—even the seasoned pros saw that.

When primary day came, Jack overwhelmed his nine opponents. Even his most ardent supporters were surprised with the vote he amassed. But Jack was philosophical about it.

"Timing means almost everything in politics," he told reporters later. "I was elected because I was the only veteran in the race, and if my brother Joe hadn't been killed, he would have been the Congressman."

Such self-depreciation wasn't deserved. However, that was the way Jack looked at things. As far as he was concerned, there always could be improvements. Jack

was on his way to success, but he always maintained
the feeling that he wasn't the only one responsible for it.

"Just as I went into politics because Joe died," Jack
would tell interviewers, "if anything happened to me
tomorrow, my brother Bobby would run. . . . and if
Bobby died, Teddy would take over for him."

XII

Senator Kennedy and the Senator's Lady

ONE BRIGHT fall afternoon, the Medford, Mass., high-school football team was joined by a lanky recruit wearing a faded uniform. Halfback Freddy Greenleaf spotted the newcomer and yelled, "Hey, kid, come over here and shag some passes." The new man did as he was told. He caught some passes. He also tossed a few. Then, breathing heavily, he ran down some punts.

Coach John Prior, spotting the activity, ambled over and asked: "How's the Congressman doing, Freddy?"

"Is that what they call him, coach?" replied the halfback. "He needs a lot of work. What year's he in?"

Chuckling, the coach introduced Freddy to his pass-catching Congressman, John Kennedy, who had come to the high school to visit an old friend.

This incident really happened, but when Jack Kennedy first went to Washington as a Congressman, fictitious stories spread overnight about how the youthful legislator was mistaken for a Senate page boy. Though such stories weren't true, nobody could deny that Jack didn't look at all like a Congressman.

At 29, Jack was many years younger than most of his

fellow Congressmen. And the shock of brown hair, tilting precariously over his unfurrowed forehead, gave many people the impression that he had just graduated from college. Jack set about dispelling that notion as fast as he could. Unlike some of his colleagues, who wavered between their promises and deeds, Jack set out to serve his constituents in Boston in the fashion he had promised to do. In return, he won re-election to his Congressional seat in 1948 and again in 1950. He learned the ins and outs of Washington's complicated political life and his popularity in his home state grew with each successive re-election.

Jack had a "safe seat"—one that could never be seriously challenged, but it soon became obvious to him that unless he pushed ahead, he could stagnate in Congress. What should he do? Which way should he turn? Should he run for the governorship of Massachusetts, or should he seek a larger role in national politics.

Without any clear path ahead, Jack began running hard again. Baseball players have a saying that the best players make their own luck. They keep plugging ahead, spending extra hours in the batting cage, or trying to learn how to catch twisting fly balls hit into the sun, or perfecting a new pitch with which they can surprise a batter at a crucial moment. Kennedy was like a ball player, always trying to increase his skills. He'd work hard during the week at his chores in Congress, but when the weekends rolled around and everyone else would take time off, Jack would fly back to Massachusetts to give speeches and talk to voters— even though he had no specific goal in mind.

Jack kept up his relentless schedule in the early 1950's. And when the opportunity arose to better himself, Jack was ready. He decided to run for the Senate.

Again the decision was a bold one. But analyzed by
Jack's cool, dispassionate eye, it seemed wise. As one
of the 435 members of Congress, Jack was not, and
probably would never be very important on the national
or world scene. But in the upper house, where the
number of Senators was small, his chances for eminence
and responsibility were that much greater.

Jack's target for 1952 was the Senatorial seat held by
Henry Cabot Lodge. It would be a tough battle Jack
reasoned, but with his extra years of campaigning in
almost all the state's 351 cities and towns behind him,
he believed he had a good chance of winning. At least
he wasn't entering the race as an unknown, as he had
in his first Congressional race in 1946.

In challenging Lodge, Jack was also challenging
the enormous popularity of the Republican candidate
for President in 1952, Dwight D. Eisenhower, a strong
supporter of Lodge's. Lodge had been one of the early
leaders in the movement to get Eisenhower to run
for President, and, furthermore, Lodge had agreed to
serve as Ike's campaign manager in the 1952 Presidential campaign.

But Lodge's working for Eisenhower meant that he
would have to cut down somewhat on his own efforts
for re-election. Jack quickly saw the flaw and began to
turn it to his own use, stepping up his campaign to a
pitch that Lodge couldn't hope to match. This accel-
erated pace of politicking took its toll on Jack as well—
his back was hurting severely again, and he had to
campaign on crutches for a while. But he drove himself furiously and kept his pain to himself.

One by one, Jack smoothed out the problems facing
him. But what he still needed was a strong device that
would forge a lasting bond between himself and the

voters. One idea after another was dreamed up, discussed, and rejected. Finally he decided to use a variation of the open houses that had made him so popular when he first ran for Congress. With the fervor displayed by Bostonians of old, Jack and his aides initiated a new version of the tea party to throw Lodge out of office.

For the plan to be successful, however, the other members of the family had to join in, and they were quick to answer the call. One after the other, they arrived in Boston to put on a show of solidarity that could only be achieved by the dynamic Kennedy family. Sisters Jean and Eunice flew in from Chicago; Patricia raced up from New York. And at their head was 27-year-old Bobby, who took over the campaign and drove his family and other workers mercilessly and without favoritism.

Jack's tea parties began at a crucial time. Neither candidate looked as though he had a clear-cut edge over the other, but many politicians reasoned that Lodge's close association with President Eisenhower would still be enough to give Lodge the victory. However, the parties were immediately successful, and Kennedy began to forge ahead.

Day after day, Massachusetts mailmen lugged around sleek, hand-addressed invitations to housewives across the state. One such invitation read:

Reception in honor of Mrs. Joseph P. Kennedy
and her son Congressman John F. Kennedy
Wednesday evening, October 1, 1952 at 8 o'clock
at the Commander Hotel, Cambridge, Mass.

Guests Invited

Rose Kennedy stopped the show at every party. Trim
and vigorous, she would warm up the audience by telling stories about how she had raised her nine children,
and told with a mother's concern of their sicknesses and
with a mother's pride of their accomplishments. By the
time Rose had finished, she'd awakened feelings of
pride in every mother in the room. And when Jack
finally appeared, looking handsome, though still shy and
boyish, women in the audience felt that they too had a
mother's interest in him.

Covering the election for *The New York Times*, correspondent Cabell Phillips wrote of one such party:
". . . The young Congressman said he would like each
of the ladies to come up on the stage so that he, his
mother and sister could meet them personally and have
a cup of tea with them later in the lobby. For approxi-
mately two hours an unbroken line of women filed
slowly across the stage, shaking hands with the Kennedys, mumbling confused introductions and pleasant-
ries, and pushed on through a side door into the lobby
still packed with those waiting their turn to go through
the receiving line. Along one side of the spacious room
were long tables with harassed waitresses—pouring
tea and coffee and serving cookies. (Total consumption
was reported later at 8,600 cups.) . . ."

Jack's campaign began moving faster and the Kennedys themselves never seemed to be standing still. On
election night, early returns showed Kennedy behind
Lodge, and Eisenhower ahead of the Democratic candidate for President, Adlai Stevenson. Jack was confi-
dent, however. When the votes were counted, Jack
found himself the winner by a 70,000-vote margin. The
most remarkable aspect of the election was that Eisenhower had carried the state by 208,000 votes in his

Presidential race against Adlai Stevenson. Jack had reversed the trend, not only beating Lodge, but Eisenhower's popularity, in winning his seat in the Senate.

After the election, when reporters were asking him how he believed he had won the campaign, Jack disclosed that he had worn a good luck campaign button on his suit on election day. The button had been struck in 1912, and it bore a picture of his grandfather, John F. Fitzgerald, who was then running for the office of mayor of Boston. It brought Jack luck, all right—the luck of the Irish!

Jack returned to Washington as a Senator, a handsome 35-year-old bachelor, considered one of the most attractive "catches" in the nation. While the society columnists carefully noted his every public appearance, he quietly resumed dating a young lady he'd met a year earlier: Jacqueline Lee Bouvier.

Only a girl like Jackie could hope to capture Jack's heart. She was exquisitely beautiful, as slender as a fashion model, with an easy-going charm and a warm personality. She excelled in sports, and was also a talented artist, a brilliant conversationalist, and an avid reader of the classics.

Such a combination of grace, beauty and intelligence proved to be bachelor Kennedy's undoing. Jack had met Jacqueline at a small dinner party, and, recalling the incident later, he admits that he was attracted to her immediately. "I leaned across the asparagus," Jack says, "and asked for a date."

Their first dates had been haphazard, with Jack constantly on the move, campaigning across Massachusetts in his free time. But, in 1952 when he returned to

Washington as a Senator, Jack began another serious campaign—this one to win Jackie's hand.

At the time, Jackie was working as the inquiring photographer for the *Washington Times-Herald.* She'd interview people throughout the city, asking for their opinions on almost every subject imaginable and snap their pictures with a cumbersome Speed Graphic she'd learned to use with close to professional skill.

But during the evenings, the journalist and the Senator would slip off to dinner and the movies. And soon, young Senator Kennedy proposed and Jackie accepted. They were married in September, 1953 in St. Mary's Roman Catholic Church in Newport, Rhode Island, by an old family friend, The Most Reverend Richard J. Cushing, then the Archbishop of Boston. It was the wedding of the year, and a crowd of 1,200 people—many of them fellow Senators and Congressmen—were on hand to wish the bride and groom good fortune and happiness.

Everything seemed to be working out beautifully. The bride and groom honeymooned in Mexico. When they returned to Washington, they purchased a lovely Virginia home and began planning for a big family.

But fate was to interfere.

XIII

A Profile in Courage

POLITICS is a cruel profession that demands that the man who masters it stay astride it as if he were riding a bucking horse. Jack found himself busier than ever; his new duties as Senator called for more and more time on his part. This in itself he could cope with, for while the work was long and hard, it was also exhilarating and meaningful.

By rights, the newly married Kennedys should have slipped into an easy and gracious family life. Their large new home in Virginia was the ideal place to raise a large family, a place where children could be brought up in a warm world of family love.

There was, however, one problem that he was unable to master. His old back injury—the ruptured disc he'd suffered at Harvard which had been aggravated again when the Japanese destroyer had rammed his PT-Boat —was acting up. Day after day the agony increased and little lines of pain began to show around the corners of his eyes.

The pain of an injured back is excruciating. A man's spine is a vulnerable and delicate housing for the nerves that serve his body. Damage to the spine can

128

cause crushed or pinched nerves. The resulting pain is
constant, never-ending, and fills a person with a stom-
ach-turning agony. Slowly but surely, Jack found his
physical condition deteriorating. Every step brought a
new wave of pain. Finally, he had to appear in Congress on crutches.

The young Senator had fought hard against letting
friends know the true extent of his suffering. The campaign for the Senate had tested his self-control to the
utmost and there had been days when only a bath in almost boiling hot water could relax the muscle spasms
near his injured spine. Only after he acknowledged
that he could no longer manage without crutches, did
the stories of the suffering he had undergone begin to
spread among his colleagues.

The original operation Jack had undergone while he
was in the Navy had failed to heal properly. A metal
plate that the Navy surgeons had attached to his spine
to make it stronger had, for some unknown reason,
failed to do the job completely.

"You could look into a hole in Jack's back and actually
see the plate the surgeons had put there," said one of
his friends. "Some days during the 1952 campaign, Jack
couldn't move without crutches, and he hated to be
seen by the public using them. When we'd come to the
door of a hall where Jack was going to give a speech,
he'd hand the crutches to one of us at the door, throw
his shoulders back, and walk down the aisle with his
back as straight as a West Point cadet's. I'll never know
how he did it."

Now, even will power couldn't keep the pain from
affecting his activities. Once, a friend went to visit Jack
at Hyannis Port and found him sitting on the porch,
punching his crutches with a deep frustration. "I'd

rather die than spend the rest of my life on these things,"
Jack said to his friend.

Here he was, handicapped by his body once again.
He had licked the problem of being underweight when
he was a child; he had again built up his body in order
to get into the Navy; he had pulled his crew away from
death in the South Pacific despite his own injuries; he
loved, and was proficient at, all forms of outdoor physical activity. Now, he thought gloomily, it looked as
though he might have to spend the remainder of his
life using crutches and suffering constant pain.

It was another challenge—probably more dangerous
than the ones he'd faced before—but it was a challenge
to be met and conquered. Jack knew that if his condition worsened—and it was bound to—he would probably have to give up his political career. And so, with the
same deliberation that led him to take the risk of de-
serting the sagging hull of his sinking PT-Boat, Jack decided to stake everything on an operation to heal his
back.

Although Kennedy wanted to go ahead with an operation, his doctors couldn't agree. They postponed the
operation again and again as they made one series of
tests after another. Some doctors frankly urged Jack
not to risk surgery. His life would be in danger, they
said, and they quoted long odds against his living
through the operation.

But Jack was adamant. He would not live his life as a
cripple if he could help it. The operation would take
place. Finally in October of 1954, a team of surgeons
began the delicate task of a double fusion of the discs
in Jack's spine.

The operation presented Jack with a new test of

courage. A spinal fusion leaves a person in a depressed state of mind and the pain is cruel.

He lay immobile for weeks after the operation. He couldn't sit up to read and because of this, the hospital room was kept dark all the time. Even when he wanted to sleep, he couldn't. Nurses would wake him up every 30 minutes to take blood tests to make sure that no infection was starting. Another medical problem was Jack's poorly functioning adrenal glands. These crucial organs, which are supposed to produce a defense against shock and infection, had been strained during his struggle in the South Pacific. Now, when he needed all the protection he could get from the vital adrenalin, he was barely getting enough.

Jacqueline stayed by her husband's side through this period, nursing him, doing everything she could to take his mind off his pain. Once, while Jackie was present, Jack received a blood transfusion and suddenly began to react violently to the fresh supply of blood dripping into his veins. His face began swelling and puffing and Jackie watched, horrified by this new suffering of the man she loved.

On two occasions, Jack's condition sank so swiftly doctors summoned the family to his bedside because they feared Jack was dying. But somewhere deep inside himself, Jack found a last bit of will to live and pulled himself back from the brink of death.

As Christmas approached in 1954 Jack was still immobile in his bed and was getting no better. His morale was dropping now and the doctors, hopeful that a change of scene would do him good, bundled him up on a stretcher and let him fly off to Palm Beach to spend Christmas with the large Kennedy family. But even the warmth of Florida and a family Christmas didn't help. The wound did not heal and in February he returned to the hospital for still another operation. The last rites of the Catholic Church were said again for Jack before he was wheeled into the operating room. And while the family prayed outside, a team of surgeons labored for hours removing the metal plate that had been fastened to Jack's spine.

This time the operation was successful, and the family and Jack rejoiced. There were still painful months in bed to come, but his back was healing and his strength slowly returned. Finally, with a triumphant grin, he walked out of the hospital to go home for a long period of convalescence. His back would never be perfect, he would always be subject to some small attacks of discomfort, but never, his doctors said, would he suffer to such an extent again. It was close to a clean bill of health. Jack had courageously fought a battle against sickness. He had gambled his life for his health—and won. It was a giddy feeling.

Jack couldn't return to the Senate for some time. His back was getting better, but wasn't yet strong enough to stand the rigors of political life. His doctors prescribed several months of inactivity. While most people would have rejoiced that such a serious operation had been successful and would have relaxed for a while, Jack found that he was unable to lie still, day after day, doing nothing. His thoughts began to center on a specific subject.

His war experiences, his political experiences and, now, his medical experiences, had made him aware that courage was not a simple thing, nor did it always take the same form. There seemed to be almost as many kinds of courage as there were kinds of men; but whatever form it took, it was a good and brave thing. As his thoughts took shape he found himself intrigued with the subject of political courage—where men would risk everything to stand fast to a principle they believed in.

Jack's interest in political courage went back to his college days when he had written *Why England Slept* and depicted the failings of British politicians in not alerting their nation to the threat of Nazism. Now with time on his hands, he delved deeper, ordering cartons of books from the Library of Congress. His Senate aide, Theodore Sorensen, scoured Washington for anecdotes and factual material about the courageous political decisions made by early American statesmen. Slowly, with Jack writing the first draft in laborious longhand from his bed, a book began to take shape.

Jack called his new book *Profiles in Courage,* and it won immediate acclaim for the young Senator. It was written with a newspaperman's sharp eye for detail, picturing the supreme efforts of many great Americans. Here was Sam Houston, the first President of the Republic of Texas who, later, as Governor of the state, fought against Texas' secession from the Union. Here, too, was Daniel Webster, whose fiery temperament and love of country led him to risk political suicide to fight for the preservation of the United States—only to die, embittered and alone. And here was Edmund G. Ross, an almost forgotten Senator from Kansas, who refused to vote for the impeachment of President Andrew Johnson, and thereby knowingly put an end to his own political career. It was all there, the tales of decision that changed the course of history and the bitter choices men had to make to follow the guide of their conscience. The book climbed to the best-seller lists and soon won

Jack the nation's highest literary award, the coveted
Pulitzer Prize. Later, the book was re-edited for a children's edition, and once again it was a best-seller.

Profiles in Courage also catapulted Jack into the
national spotlight as a Senator extraordinary. He was
no longer a young Senator fresh from the seashore of
Massachusetts. He had proved himself in battle. He
had won his political fights. He had conquered a grave
threat to his health. And now, he had also made his
mark as a prize-winning author of a significant and
noteworthy book on politics.

"When a politician loves neither the public good nor
himself," Jack had written, "or when his love for himself is limited by the trappings of office, then the public's interest is badly served. But when his regard for
himself is so high that his own self-respect demands he
follow the path of courage and conscience, all benefit . . . Thus, in the days ahead, only the very courageous will be able to make the hard and unpopular decisions necessary for our survival in the struggle with a
powerful enemy—an enemy with leaders who need give
little thought to the popularity of their course, who
need pay little tribute to the public opinion they themselves manipulate, and who may force, without fear of
retaliation at the polls, their citizens to sacrifice present
laughter for future glory. And only the courageous will
be able to keep alive the spirit of individualism and
dissent which gave birth to this nation, nourished it as
an infant and carried it through its severest tests upon
the attainment of its maturity."

Might the Senator's words have personal meaning?
As one book reviewer put it: "Such a book is something
more than a record of the past; it is a challenge to the

future. It sets high standards for Senator Kennedy himself."

As Jack took his place in the Senate again, only one thought could have been deep in his mind, a thought he would not yet dare to put in words. Now he must move forward, trying to live up to the standards he had established for himself. If successful, they would lead him to one inevitable conclusion—a try for the Presidency of the United States.

XIV

Saved from the
Vice-Presidency

IT IS TRUE that Kennedy's prize-winning book had
gained for him a certain national stature. Further, soon
after his return to action in 1954 he quickly earned the
grudging approval of fellow Senators as he proved himself a capable legislator. As his reputation in Washington grew, informed newspapers began calling Jack one
of the most able and dynamic young men to appear in
the Senate in many years.

For all this, however, on the broad national scene
where the average citizen and his vote determine the
course of American history—Kennedy was still basically unknown. Here, in early 1956, at the grass-roots of
American life, there were few active politicians whose
names were known to all: Eisenhower, Nixon, Stevenson, Johnson, Rayburn, Kefauver and perhaps a small
handful of others. Although insiders would point out
that young Jack Kennedy seemed headed for bigger
things, he was still a far cry from real national promi-
nence.

Paradoxically, John F. Kennedy would become a na-
tionally known politician only by suffering a defeat.

Early in 1956, in his home state of Massachusetts, Jack had flexed his growing political muscles and come up with effective control of the 16 votes Massachusetts would cast at the Democratic National Convention.

Now, it was June, and in Chicago thousands of Democrats from all across the nation gathered to draft a platform and to choose their candidates for President and Vice-President. There was only small doubt that Adlai Stevenson, the balding, intellectual former Governor of Illinois would again win the nomination as the Democratic candidate for President. Stevenson had been nominated in 1952, run against Eisenhower, and lost. If he were to run again, he'd need a new partner for the Vice-Presidency and Jack was being mentioned in many places as an ideal man to fill the bill.

Although advice was plentiful, Jack refused to commit himself. His father was adamant in his feelings that Jack should not try for the Vice-Presidency, arguing that Stevenson was bound to lose to Eisenhower as he had four years earlier and Jack would be defeated with him. Jack's aides, on the other hand, argued that Jack ought to run because Stevenson could win and even if he didn't, it would place Kennedy on the national scene at a time when he needed the publicity. Finally, Jack decided he'd run—if he could get the nomination.

And so, Jack journeyed to Chicago with the knowledge that he was one of the contenders for the Vice-Presidential nomination. True, he had no clear-cut commitment that he would be Stevenson's choice as a running mate. But, then again, according to press reports, no one else had such a commitment either.

Stevenson certainly had been cordial to Kennedy. On the other hand, the Governor was an outspoken liberal, and some liberal Democrats were still displeased with

Kennedy's refusal to come out vehemently against Senator Joseph McCarthy in the early 1950's. On the other side of the coin, however, were other Kennedy positions taken in Congress, which were growing increasingly more liberal. Now, in Chicago, the big question for Jack was, "Is Stevenson for me or against me?" This was the crucial question, for, in the past, the Presidential nominee usually had the last word in the choice of a running mate.

It was against this tense backdrop that, about 12 hours before the nominations were to start, Jack received a call from Governor Stevenson. Would Kennedy make the nominating speech for Stevenson? Yes, certainly, yes he would, Kennedy answered.

It was a stunning blow. Its meaning, guessed Jack, was fairly clear: the man who made the nominating speech was merely being tossed a bone to build his self-respect. Then, later, the candidate could overlook him in choosing his Vice-Presidential running mate. It was a device as old as the hills, and as Jack stood before the convention, praising Stevenson and giving the reasons why Stevenson should be nominated, thoughts about his own future coursed through his mind. Was Stevenson really giving him the brush-off? Why had he been picked to give the nominating speech? There was no answer to be read on the thousands of upturned faces staring back at him through clouds of cigarette and cigar smoke.

Later, Jack met with a delegation from New England and honestly confessed his lack of hope of winning second spot on the ticket. The delegates crowded around him. "Does that mean you're withdrawing from the race?" they asked, worried expressions on their faces. "No," Jack replied, explaining that while he felt the situation wasn't hopeful, he wasn't going to concede either.

Though Jack didn't know it, the situation was about to break wide open. Stevenson won the nomination the next day, and made a dramatic statement. In a break with precedent, he declared that there would be an open race for the Vice-Presidential nomination. All the men mentioned were acceptable to him. May the best man win. Delegates were astounded by the sudden turn of events. The nomination was up for grabs and the scramble was on for the prize.

That night, Chicago was a madhouse. Jack and his aides put on a last-minute drive to corral the pledges necessary to win the Vice-Presidential nomination. Contact men were busy trying to run down delegates who had either gone to bed or were out celebrating throughout the city. It was a long night, filled with frustrations, moments of hope and moments of despair.

When the balloting began the following day, Jack found himself locked in battle with Senator Estes Kefauver of Tennessee. Sitting calmly in front of his hotel room television set, Jack watched the struggle taking place on the crowded floor of the convention hall. As the TV cameras picked up the scene of hastily whispered conferences between political leaders, he rapidly evaluated the strength of his situation but kept his feelings carefully to himself. His aides and associates were excited, but Kennedy was calm and detached. He would take a relaxing bath, he said.

On the second ballot, Jack began picking up votes. New York decided to go with Kennedy; Texas swung to him, too. Jack needed just 68 more votes to win; the nomination was but a hairsbreadth away and his aides began to shout excitedly. Jack left his tub to watch and when Kentucky threw him another 30 votes, Ted Sorensen moved to shake Jack's hand. "Congratulations, Jack," Sorensen said. "That's it."

"No, not yet," Jack replied and he turned to watch the TV set. What had he spotted that had slipped by the others?

Whatever it was, a hunch, or a knowledge of how other states would react to his candidacy, Jack had spotted a shift. Moments later the convention broke toward Kefauver and Jack watched silently as his opponent's votes piled up. There could be no stopping Kefauver now. Jack knew this, but no disappointment showed on his face. The convention was a whirlpool of confusion. Then, as Kefauver picked up the last few votes he needed for victory, Jack turned to his aides. "Let's go," he said quietly.

Dressing with the same careful deliberation he had shown in the last few hours, Jack prepared to go to the convention hall. He had suffered the first defeat of his political career. It never showed. He entered the convention with a grin, as though he had won, not lost, and pushing his way to the rostrum, Jack stood erect and handsome before the crowd. He thanked all the people who had worked so hard for him, then asked that a final vote be taken and Kefauver's nomination be made unanimous.

Jack's appearance turned the defeat into a personal victory. His polished and gracious speech left a striking impact of a young man who would be heard from in the future. Millions of Americans watching the proceedings over television were impressed by Jack's spirit at such a crucial moment. He might have lost the nomination, but his actions had proved he was ready for the major leagues.

Remarkably, the loss turned out to be beneficial. As Jack's father had predicted, Stevenson and Kefauver were swamped by the popularity of President Eisenhower in the November, 1956, election. Jack had escaped defeat in a national election. If he had run with Stevenson, a large share of the defeat would have rested on his shoulders, hampering his future chances of running for higher office. Worse yet, because Jack was a Catholic, his defeat could have been interpreted as a signal that the nation was not yet ready to elect a Catholic to so high an office. As younger brother Bobby would later refer to the incident, it was the time "Jack was saved from the Vice-Presidency."

After the convention, Kennedy followed up by campaigning diligently and effectively for the Stevenson-Kefauver ticket. And wherever he campaigned, he was greeted with enthusiasm by the citizens of America who a few short months ago had not known of his existence. After Stevenson's loss, Jack found that his new popularity had raised him from the status of a questionable Vice-Presidential candidate to that of a front runner for the biggest prize of all—the Presidency. And he began running hard.

XV

At Home with the Kennedys

LEST ANYONE think that during this time the life of the entire Kennedy family centered solely on politics and hard work, it is necessary to submit one item of evidence. From it, one may glean that if the irrepressible tribe of Kennedys had grown older, they had not grown any less irrepressible or any less competitive.

After one rugged weekend at the Kennedy home at Hyannis Port an anonymous guest, who had suffered the entire time from the constant exercise, drew up a set of rules for future visitors. Titled "What to Expect When Visiting the Kennedys," they go like this:

> "The following ought to be placed under the pillows of each new guest and some of the old ones who may have forgotten. It should be read carefully. Failure to do so may cause you painful embarrassment.

> ### AT THE DINNER TABLE

> "Prepare yourself by reading *The Congressional Record, U.S. News & World Report,*

142

Time, Newsweek, Fortune, The Nation, The Democratic Digest, The Ensign, and the manual, 'How to Play Sneaky Tennis.' Memorize page 2 of 'Jokes Guaranteed to Lay Them in the Aisles.' Anticipate that each Kennedy will ask you what you think of another Kennedy's (a) dress, (b) hairdo, (c) backhand, (d) latest achievement. You will find that 'Terrific!' is a satisfactory answer. They won't listen to much detail.

WHAT TO EXPECT ON THE FOOTBALL FIELD

"It's touch football, but it's murder. The only way I know of to get out of playing is not to come at all, or to come with a broken leg. If you don't have a broken leg, and if you come, you will play; that is, you will if you don't want to take your supper in the kitchen or if you want to talk to anyone for the rest of the weekend.

"It is wise to know some football terms. The girls drop words like 'button hook,' 'two-on-one' and 'stop-and-go' with ease, as though they were sitting around the Harvard locker room—and I'm sure that when the weekend is over, you will feel that you have spent most of your time there. You will be wise not to suggest plays even though you were a star quarterback at school or college. The Kennedys have the play-calling department all sewed up and all of them have received A-plus in leadership. If you see one make a mistake here and there, keep still—but never stand still. Run madly on all plays even if you weren't lucky enough to be signaled out in a huddle to carry out a mysterious assignment.

"Make a lot of noise and make out you never had a better time in your life. Things will go smoother if you do. Don't overdo this, though. Don't make out you're having altogether too much fun. If you do, you'll be accused of not taking the game seriously enough.

"Look glum if your team doesn't score a touchdown and become gleeful when your team does. Don't criticize your teammates. (It's a team game.) And for goodness sake don't harp on any error of the enemy, because the enemy will be made up of Kennedys, too, and the Kennedys don't like that sort of thing.

"If you want to become popular, show raw guts. They like this. To show raw guts is not an easy thing to do, but it will help if you fall on your face after every play. It also looks good if you smash into the house going after a pass. That shows you are really trying. They like to see you playing on a twisted ankle or shrugging off a hole in your best suit. Simple things like that will help your game enormously. I know that it sounds incredible and that they might take the game a little seriously, but it's true; and, oh Yes! Don't be too good. Let Jack run around you every so often. It will be tough to fake, but it is a wise thing to try.

"Don't under any circumstances, let Ethel fool you. Never treat her . . . as a woman. Her husband has spent all his spare time developing her change of pace, her timing

Newport, Rhode Island, September, 1953. The wedding of the year. The bride is the former Jacqueline Lee Bouvier.

Jack and Jackie on vacation at Hyannis Port.   *U.P.I.*

Breakfast at home with the Kennedys.

October, 1954: On crutches, Senator Kennedy enters New York Hospital for Special Surgery.   *U.P.I.*

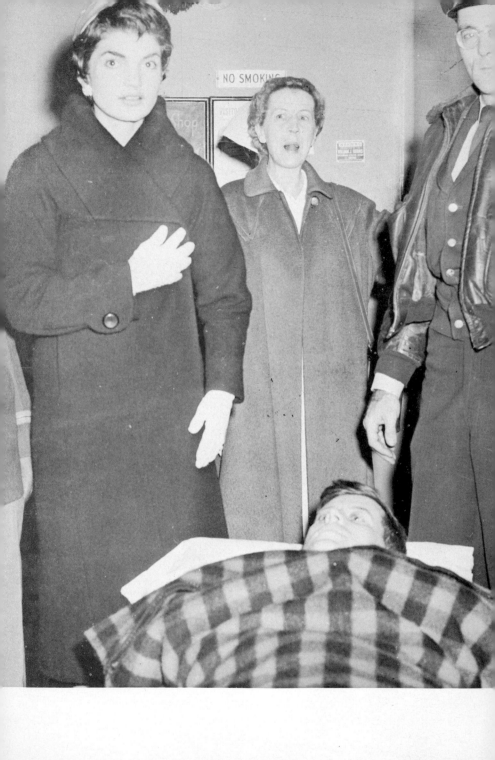

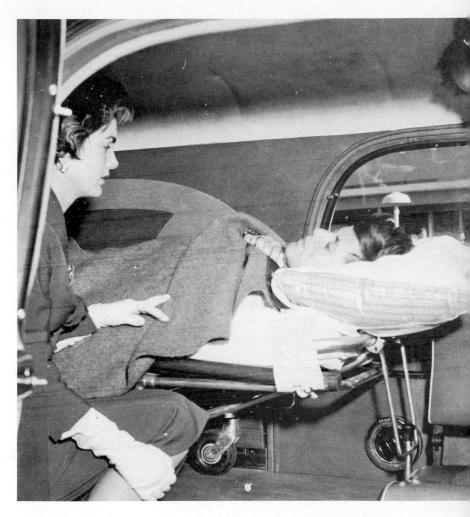

Above and left, Christmas, 1954: Kennedy is taken by stretcher, ambulance and plane from the hospital in New York to Palm Beach, Florida, to spend holidays with his family.

U.P.I.

THE TRUSTEES OF COLUMBIA UNIVERSITY
IN THE CITY OF NEW YORK
TO ALL PERSONS TO WHOM THESE PRESENTS MAY COME GREETING
BE IT KNOWN THAT

JOHN F . KENNEDY
has been awarded
THE PULITZER PRIZE IN LETTERS
- BIOGRAPHY -
FOR "PROFILES IN COURAGE"

IN ACCORDANCE WITH THE PROVISIONS OF THE STATUTES OF THE
UNIVERSITY GOVERNING SUCH AWARD
IN WITNESS WHEREOF WE HAVE CAUSED THIS CERTIFICATE TO BE
SIGNED BY THE PRESIDENT OF THE UNIVERSITY AND OUR CORPORATE
SEAL TO BE HERETO AFFIXED IN THE CITY OF NEW YORK ON THE
SIXTH   DAY OF   MAY   IN THE YEAR OF
OUR LORD ONE THOUSAND NINE HUNDRED AND FIFTY SEVEN

PRESIDENT

The Pulitzer Prize.

Senator Kennedy nominates Adlai Stevenson for the Presidency at the 1956 Democratic National Convention.

1957: Bobby Kennedy, counsel to the special Senate Committee investigating labor racketeering, huddles with brother Jack, a member of the Committee.   *U.P.I.*

1959: Brother Teddy, center, a recent law school graduate, joins brothers Bobby and Jack for a conference during a pause in rackets hearings.   *U.P.I.*

Jackie, Jack and daughter Caroline.   *Jacques Lowe*

Jacques Lowe

Above: The nomination is secure—victory at Los Angeles Convention, 1960. Below: Campaigning in New York with wife Jackie in open car.

Cecil Layne

The campaign moves into high gear.   *Jacques Lowe*

Beatrice O'Conlin

With Democratic leaders. From left: Senator Stuart Symington, former President Harry S. Truman, Kennedy, Senator
Hubert Humphrey.   *Jacques Lowe*

Planning campaign strategy. From left: Vice-Presidential
candidate Lyndon Johnson, campaign manager Bobby Kennedy, Presidential candidate John Kennedy.   *Jacques Lowe*

A crucial television debate with opponent Richard M. Nixon.

The closing days of the 1960 campaign.   *Walter B. Morse*

Enroute to the White House during the Inaugural Parade.

The oath of office is administered by Chief Justice Earl Warren, January 20, 1961.

on reverses, her endurance, and so forth, and she will make you look silly. My best advice to you is not to come at all; or if you do, rest your broken leg on a railing and cheer wildly for Bobby's team."

XVI

The Early Fight for the Presidency

"No CATHOLIC, however capable he might be, could be elected to the Presidency of our land at the present day."

So spoke one of the nation's leading Catholic theologians only 14 years before Sen. John Kennedy made his bid to become President of the United States. In 1960, many Americans still believed this—a Catholic could never be elected to the White House.

Only once before, 32 years earlier, a Catholic had run for President—and had lost decisively. That was New York's Al Smith. However, some politicians, cautiously testing the public sentiment in 1960, advanced the theory that there was now less bigotry in America. This, of course, was difficult to prove for in certain sections of the land there still seemed to be an overwhelming groundswell of public opinion violently opposed to the election of a Catholic President.

Kennedy realized he would have a tough road to travel if he were to win even the nomination, let alone the Presidency itself. There were many problems he faced. One, obviously, was religion. Another was age

162

—if he won, he'd be the youngest man ever elected to the Presidency. A third problem was his position as Senator—only one other man, Warren Harding, had been elected President directly from a Senate seat. By the very nature of his job, a Senator was forced to make unpopular decisions—and unpopular decisions lose votes. Summing it all up several years before he started the final campaign, Jack told a reporter: "Nobody is going to hand me the nomination. If I were a governor of a large state, Protestant, and 55, I could sit back and let it come to me. But if I am going to get the nomination, I'll have to work for it—and darned hard."

Comparing Jack with Al Smith, there were many differences. Al Smith had been born in the slums of the lower east side of New York City, and had fought his way to success through a poverty-stricken world. He spoke with a New York accent, and to America's rural population he presented the image of a fast-talking city slicker. Although he was a capable, honest politician, he was identified by association with the corrupt practices of New York's powerful political organization, Tammany Hall.

By contrast, Jack Kennedy was as different from Al Smith as any candidate could be. Kennedy was a Catholic, yes, but he was also a millionaire; he had been educated in the finest schools in the world; he was lean and handsome; he was an intellectual, an author and a voracious reader of significant books; he had a war record that would have done justice to a Hollywood thriller and, quite importantly, he had a voting record in the Senate of helping labor and the poor while maintaining a conservative balance on other issues. In political terms, Jack's background was unbeatable.

His age was, Jack admitted, a problem. But if the

Republicans were to nominate 47-year-old Vice-President Richard M. Nixon, his 43 years wouldn't seem so young at all.

Viewing the situation as objectively as possible, John Kennedy thought he had an outside chance for the nomination, if he could prove to his party and to America that he was unquestionably the finest candidate available. Accordingly, years before the first presidential primary election, Jack started his campaign. Quickly, he assembled a young, aggressive staff and began accepting speaking engagements all over the country. As in his 1952 race for the Senate, and his 1946 campaign for the House, he would start early and keep fighting.

Almost immediately, he found himself embroiled with every thorny political problem of the day.

One controversial issue was segregation, a subject so touchy that Jack had been advised not even to mention it. In 1958, mobs had overwhelmed the sleepy Southern city of Little Rock, Arkansas, in protest against the decision that the Little Rock schools, which had been restricted to white students in the past, should now open their doors to Negro students as well. President Eisenhower ordered the Army into the city to retain order, and Southerners were violently opposed to what they considered high-handed tactics on the part of the Federal government.

Jack was advised not to go into the South during this time of crisis. His advisors pointed out that if he said anything friendly to the Southerners to assuage their hurt feelings, the liberals of the North would be angered. On the other hand, if Jack came out strongly against segregation, the Southerners obviously would turn against him—and Jack had received strong support from the South in his 1956 campaign for Vice-President, and needed it again in 1960 to get the Presidential nomination.

This bothered Jack, but it didn't stop him. He had fought too often for causes that people considered too hot to handle. For example, he had urged curbs on labor unions which angered both Republicans and Democrats—the Republicans because Jack's proposals weren't harsh enough, the Democrats because the proposals were hard on labor and the Democrats had always been friends of labor. Furthermore, Jack had accepted a speaking engagement in Mississippi long before the Little Rock riots broke out. Now he wasn't going to let the possibility of his getting in trouble stop him from going there.

When he arrived in Mississippi, the local newspapers carried a challenge from the state's Republican Chairman, Wirt Yeager, Jr., daring Jack to state his views on school integration when he made his speech that evening. That night, Jack faced an expectant audience. His initial remarks were met by silence. Then, swinging from the heels, he met Yeager's challenge head on. "I have no hesitancy in telling the Republican chairman the same thing I told my own city of Boston," Jack said, his eyes aglitter, "that I accept the Supreme Court decision as the supreme law of the land. I think most of us agree on the necessity to uphold law and order in all parts of the country."

Jack paused, the room grew quiet. Then Jack continued, "And now, I challenge the local Republican Chairman to tell us where he stands on Eisenhower and Nixon!"

The crowd broke into spontaneous applause and cheers. Accounts of the occasion include the remarks of a local Congressman, who told a reporter, "I never thought I'd see anybody in central Mississippi speak up for integration and get a standing ovation." A newsmagazine correspondent, standing close by Kennedy, heard a young Democrat tell Jack: "All these Baptists and Methodists are going to vote for you, my Catholic friend, and I'm one of them."

In calling Jack "my Catholic friend," the young Democrat pinpointed one of the biggest stumbling blocks Jack faced. He might be running for the Presidency, but he was considered the "Catholic candidate," or the "Catholic office-seeker," or the "man who wants to be the first Catholic President." There was no separation between Jack and his religion in the eyes of many voters. Their ancient bias against Catholicism made them feel that Kennedy's religion would keep him from upholding the Constitution properly. America, they said, stood for complete separation of church and state. Catholicism did not, they continued, so we must never elect a Catholic President.

Jack faced the problem squarely. He knew his Catholicism would handicap him with some voters in a national election. But he set out to prove to the public that a Catholic, just like a Protestant or a Jew, would fully honor the Constitution should he be elected.

On one occasion, when Jack was grilled by the press, a reporter asked: "Conceivably there could be a situation in which the dictates of your Church and the demands of your country might conflict. In such a case, where would your higher loyalty lie?"

"In the first place," replied Kennedy, "I can't think of any issue where such a conflict might arise. But suppose it did? Nobody in my Church gives me orders. It doesn't work that way. I've been in Congress for ten years and it never has happened. People are afraid that Catholics take orders from a higher organization. They don't. Or at least I don't.

"Besides I can't act as a private individual does; my responsibility is to my constituents and the Constitution. So if it came to a conflict between the two, and not just a personal moral issue, I am bound to act for the interests of the many." Jack's argument carried weight. He had served honorably in Congress without conflict with his Church. He had fought in the South Pacific, and almost died, to defend the Constitution without conflict with his Church. Furthermore, Jack said, "It is the obligation of a public servant to defend the Constitution. It is *the* obligation."

XVII

The Nomination

IN NOVEMBER of 1958 John F. Kennedy was re-elected
to the Senate of the United States by 870,000 votes, the
largest plurality ever given to a Massachusetts candidate. It was a sensational victory and served to give
Kennedy an even greater stature on the national scene.

Now, his campaign for the Presidency moved into
high gear. Speaking engagements increased. His staff
grew and the pace quickened—all with one goal—the
nomination for the Presidency at the 1960 Democratic
Convention.

Bobby Kennedy, now well-known in his own right
for his fiery performance as counsel for the Senate Labor Rackets Committee (of which Jack was a member),
was devoting all of his time to Jack's campaign. Joseph
Kennedy, Sr., helped from behind the scenes using his
influence to sway New York's delegation to Jack. Teddy
helped, Pat, Jean and Eunice helped, the husbands and
wives of all the Kennedys helped. This was to be expected of course, but, soon some major national figures
joined the high-speed Kennedy bandwagon as well.
From Connecticut, Chester Bowles, Abraham Ribicoff
and John Bailey endorsed Jack. From Ohio, Governor
168

Mike Di Salle. Others, big and small from all over the country, caught the Kennedy fever.

But most important, of course, was Jack himself. Fiercely, he drove himself. Earlier one of his associates had said: "Jack's success in politics ever since his first campaign for Congress in 1946 has been entirely due to hard work and long hours. I don't think any other politician at any time ever shook so many hands in so many small villages and towns or ever shaved in the men's room of so many filling stations and bowling alleys." Well, he hadn't seen anything.

Kennedy entered every significant primary race. In Wisconsin and then in West Virginia his victories knocked Sen. Hubert Humphrey out of the race. Later primaries brought large blocs of delegates into Jack's camp. Senator Stuart Symington's bid for the nomination never got off the ground. Neither did Adlai Stevenson's. Only Senate Majority Leader Lyndon Johnson looked strong enough to present a fight at the 1960 Democratic Convention in Los Angeles.

But Johnson was toppled also as Kennedy's well-organized lieutenants scrambled around the convention floor with walkie-talkies to keep in constant touch.

On the first ballot, John F. Kennedy was nominated to be the Democratic standard-bearer in the 1960 Presidential race.

Later, at Jack's request, Johnson was nominated for the Vice-Presidency, a prize Jack himself didn't quite get just four short years earlier.

On the last day of the Convention, John F. Kennedy delivered his acceptance speech to the delegates of the convention and to the millions of Americans who were watching on television. Flushed with victory, tired from his wearying campaign, Jack's speech was rated only fair by the pundits who watched. But, no matter, he was the nominee, and there would be time to make it up.

In Washington, 3,000 miles away, another hard-working young politician was watching Kennedy deliver his "only fair" acceptance speech. The man's name was Richard M. Nixon and he was musing to himself: this guy doesn't look too tough to handle.

Two weeks later, in Chicago, Richard M. Nixon was nominated by the Republicans and the battle was drawn.

XVIII
Victory

JACK KENNEDY, at 43, the Republicans said, was too young and too inexperienced to serve capably as America's President and leader of the free world. Their man, Richard M. Nixon, was a far better choice. Nixon had served as Eisenhower's Vice-President for eight years, was older than Kennedy, was more responsible.

The Kennedy forces responded: Many of the original leaders of revolutionary America were in their early forties when this nation was first founded. President Teddy Roosevelt was only 42 when he was elevated from the Vice-Presidency upon the death of President William McKinley. Kennedy had spent as much time as Nixon in federal service in Washington—they both started out as Congressmen in 1946. America was at a crossroads—it was a time for a young, bold and imaginative President, a leader who could take us across a "New Frontier," and Jack Kennedy was that man.

The campaign began. Kennedy, and his running mate Lyndon Johnson, locked political horns with Nixon and the Republican Vice-Presidential candidate, Henry Cabot Lodge—whom Jack had beaten in the '52 Senate race in Massachusetts.

Both the Democratic and Republican platforms were

liberal documents, but the Democratic one called for greater government spending to speed up national growth and social reform. Fine ideals, retorted Nixon, but where's the money going to come from? "It's not Jack's money," he told crowds across the country, "it's *your* money." Very funny, Kennedy said in essence, but this is no joking matter. This is a great nation, but it will continue to be great only if it gets off dead center and starts moving again, at home and abroad. The extra money would itself come from national growth. We are in recession now, Jack told the crowds; we must move decisively if we are to break out of it and create jobs for the jobless.

The momentum of the campaign increased. Twelve hours of campaigning per day became 14 hours, then 16 hours, six days a week, with Sunday reserved for Church, a short rest and then more conferences, plans and strategy.

Slowly, insidiously, at first, then faster and openly vicious, the religious issue came into the campaign again, although both candidates felt it had no place there. Ugly hate literature against Catholics filled the mails, especially in the Midwest and the South. Catholic priests generally stayed out of the political arena. So did most Protestant ministers—but not all. Some openly preached from their pulpits that it would be a national disaster if a Catholic were to become President.

Jack's main counterthrust against religious bigotry found him flying to Texas to address the Greater Houston Ministerial Association. His speech was to be broadcast throughout the state on television. The challenge of the occasion, although it was never officially stated, was of such a nature that if Jack failed to convince the ministers he was capable of serving as President in the same fashion as a non-Catholic, he would win no support from this extremely powerful group.

Jack was nervous before he rose to speak. He rubbed his fists back and forth against each other, and sipped water several times during his introduction. But once he took command of the microphone, he drove directly to the heart of the matter. Reading a five-page statement, Kennedy said: "I believe in an America where the separation of church and state is absolute—where no Catholic prelate would tell the President, should he be a Catholic, how to act, and no Protestant minister would tell his parishioners how to vote. . . . I do not speak for my Church on public matters—and the Church does not speak for me."

Jack's words were driving home, and, as he approached a paragraph that would be quoted often in the future, he emphasized its meaning with sharp, dramatic chopping gestures of his right hand. "Whatever issue may come before me as President, if I should be elected—on birth control, divorce, censorship, gambling, or any other subject—I will make my decision in accordance with these views, in accordance with what my conscience tells me to be in the national interest, and without regard to outside religious pressure or dictates. And no power or threat of punishment could cause me to decide otherwise. But if the time should ever come—and I do not concede that any conflict would be even remotely possible—when my office would require me to either violate my conscience or violate the national interest, then I would resign from office, and I hope any conscientious public servant would do the same. . . ."

No one could ask Jack to say more; no one had expected him to say so much. The issue was no longer in doubt, at least as far as Jack and those who listened to his speech were concerned. The Citizens for Religious Freedom, the organization that had earlier pressed the issue, made a statement calling Jack's speech, "the most complete, unequivocal and reassuring statement that could be expected of any person in his position."·

Early in the campaign, in a dramatic move, Jack had challenged Nixon to a series of television debates, to emulate the Lincoln-Douglas debates of old. Nixon, recalling Kennedy's mediocre performance on television at the Los Angeles convention, accepted. It was Nixon's mistake.

Kennedy's challenge paid off. The first debate, in Chicago, was particularly decisive. Nixon—his heavybearded, deep-set features sweating and glowering— looked pale and pasty to the 70 million Americans who watched that first debate. His arguments were mild and unimpressive. On the other hand, Kennedy looked, and *was,* crisp, alert, sharp, clear. His finely-honed, logical analysis of America's domestic positions beamed across the country loud and clear. In one swift hour Kennedy's appearance on national television shattered Republican charges regarding his youth and immaturity. He emerged a new candidate—Jack Kennedy, young but mature, aggressive but polished, bold yet calm, intellectual but practical. He was on his way.

Another crucial incident brought Jack votes. In Atlanta, during the campaign, Negro integrationist leader Martin Luther King was arrested by city officials—for a minor traffic violation—and put in jail. Quickly, the Kennedy forces, first Jack in a personal call to Mrs.

King, then brother Bobby in a call to an Atlanta judge, indicated their sympathy to King's cause and to the cause of Negroes everywhere. The civil rights plank in the Democratic platform meant business, Kennedy showed. Nixon, hoping to get the Southern white vote, kept silent on the King issue. It was a mistake on Nixon's part, and probably contributed heavily to Nixon's loss of both the South and the great majority of Negro votes in the Northern industrial areas.

Imperceptibly at first, then more noticeably, then with a roar, Jack Kennedy's campaign took off and flew. He was mobbed by cheering throngs wherever he stopped. Influential columnists backed his candidacy. Wrote Walter Lippman, the dean of them all: ". . . It has been truly impressive to see the precision of Mr. Kennedy's mind, his immense command of the facts, his instinct for the crucial point, his singular lack of demagoguery and sloganeering, his intense concern and interest in the subject itself, the stability and steadfastness of his nerves and his coolness and his courage. And through it all have transpired the recognizable marks of the man who, besides being highly trained, is a natural leader, organizer and ruler of men." Later, *The New York Times,* frequently Republican in national elections, editorially endorsed Kennedy.

The tide had turned, the pundits said. It would be a Kennedy landslide. Still, taking no chances, Kennedy increased the pace of his campaign. Days with 18 and 20 hours of campaigning were common. Traveling constantly, by plane, train, bus and car, in a man-killing schedule, Kennedy looked fresh. His self-confidence grew and attracted still more people. He looked and talked like a winner, like a winner with a cause. "Lend me your hands and your hearts," he told the crowds, "and join me on a New Frontier."

The hardest days came when he rode in motorcades in an open convertible through the crowded streets of metropolitan areas. On one occasion, a trip through Ohio, crowds lined 113 miles of highway along Jack's route. The people held up their children to watch his passing, they broke through the police lines to touch him and clawed his arm in desperate attempts to shake his hand. His staff began to fear for his safety. Reporters accompanying the campaign wrote two or three fresh stories every day—along with the "add leads" to keep the stories up-to-date—and knew they were working hard. Jack would make as many as ten speeches a day. He wrenched and sprained his fingers with thousands of handshakes in a constant, wearying effort to greet the crush of admirers who came to pay their respects. The magnetic personality and the startling good looks of Jack Kennedy seemed to symbolize his whole "New Frontier" program to millions of Americans.

November 8, 1960. The election was not a landslide. In fact, it was the closest of the century. The Kennedy clan, all of them, watched the results tensely at their Hyannis Port home. Jack took an early lead. Then it faltered slightly. Millions of Americans all over the land stayed up well past midnight as late election returns were still being reported. From Los Angeles, at 2:00 A.M., Nixon gets on television. It looks bad, he says, but there will be no concession of defeat right now. Finally, at 10:00 the next morning Nixon concedes. John F. Kennedy has been elected President of the United States.

EPILOGUE
President-Elect

THE ELECTION is over. Suddenly, Jack Kennedy is the most powerful man in the world. Soon, by a single pen stroke, he will be able to mobilize the mighty forces of America's Army, Navy, and Air Force to send them on the attack; he can create new cities; he can destroy a continent and he can send men into space. Never in history has so much power been placed in such a young man's hands.

The next day, at Hyannis Port President-elect John F. Kennedy joins some members of his family in a little game of touch football. Going high into the air for a pass, he collides with a defensive player and falls to the ground. He gets up smiling, although his newly assigned Secret Service guards are doing anything but smiling. "That's my brother," joshes fellow-touch-football-player Bobby Kennedy, "All guts and no brains."

Before he takes office on January 20, 1961, Kennedy must build a team of men to advise him. During the months between his election and inauguration he searches for the right people who can help guide White House policy in the future. As the first snows of December sweep through Washington, he holds brief press conferences on the doorstep of his Georgetown home

177

to present the men he has chosen as his Cabinet. Here
is Dean Rusk, recently the President of the Rockefeller
Foundation, as the new Secretary of State; here also are
Robert S. McNamara, leaving his job as President of
the Ford Motor Company to become Secretary of Defense; Adlai Stevenson, who campaigned brilliantly for
Jack, is the new Ambassador to the United Nations; a
Republican, Douglas Dillon, puts his party loyalty behind his love of America and is appointed Secretary of
the Treasury; Abraham Ribicoff, formerly the Governor
of Connecticut, is the new Secretary of Health, Education and Welfare; and younger brother Bobby accepts
his elder brother's request that he serve as Attorney
General. There are many others picked by Kennedy
and they have much in common: they are surprisingly
young, very aggressive and tough, and above all, dedicated. The press delivers a verdict: Kennedy's New
Frontiersmen are the most able group ever brought to
Washington by a new President.

Despite the endless chores facing the new President-
elect, the Kennedy household in the Georgetown section of Washington retains a warmth reminiscent of the
family in which Jack was brought up. Now the father
of a young daughter named Caroline, and an infant
son, John, Jr., the Kennedy home is filled with happy
shouts as Caroline chases her kittens—"Tom Kittens"
and "Mittens"—from one room to another. Jacqueline,
adjusting to her new position as First Lady, teases her
husband lovingly if there is a sign of his being carried
away by his new importance.

Quickly, through the press, the nation learns much
about the new President. The nation learns of his avid
reading habits—how many newspapers he reads each

day (ten), how many magazines he reads regularly (16) and what books he's currently studying. The nation learns more of his strong family attachments when it is announced that the official Presidential yacht will be re-christened the *Honey Fitz*, after the new President's grandfather, one-time Mayor of Boston. Soon, the nation learns that its new President is poised, articulate, intelligent and resourceful.

And so, on a winter-whipped January day, John F. Kennedy mounts a white wooden stand in Washington and solemnly takes the oath of office as America's newest President. He delivers an inaugural speech as stirring as any in American history. Later, after leading the inaugural parade to his reviewing stand, President Kennedy stands to receive the salute of the fifty states.

What has put this man on this platform? What has made him the leader of 180 million Americans and the entire free world? The reasons are many, think those who know the young President: family solidarity; firm religious beliefs; raw courage and refined courage as well; wealth; patriotism; intelligence and intellect; ambition; vigor, drive and industry. It is all of these things and it is more; it is a belief in growth and in one's self— that a man can be what he aspires to be if he can grow and improve as he grows. "We all stayed the same after we graduated," said a Kennedy Harvard classmate, "but Jack never stopped growing."

The Navy's float—a real-life 75-ton PT-Boat with "*PT-109*" markings on its hull—goes slowly by the reviewing stand, carrying the surviving members of Kennedy's original crew through the dazzling afternoon sun. What thoughts are in Kennedy's mind? His fight with death in the South Pacific? His bed-ridden agony as he fought to walk again? His childhood days of sailing with his brother Joe, who can't be present to share his honor today? All this flashes back, then disappears. The future lies ahead.

APPENDIX

John F. Kennedy's First Inaugural Address

Delivered at the U. S. Capitol, Jan. 20, 1961:

MY FELLOW CITIZENS:

We observe today not a victory of party but a celebration of freedom—symbolizing an end as well as a beginning—signifying renewal as well as change. For I have sworn before you and Almighty God the same solemn oath our forebears prescribed nearly a century and three quarters ago.

The world is very different now. For man holds in his mortal hands the power to abolish all form of human poverty and to abolish all form of human life. And, yet, the same revolutionary beliefs for which our forebears fought are still at issue around the globe—the belief that the rights of man come not from the generosity of the state but from the hand of God.

We dare not forget today that we are the heirs of that first revolution. Let the word go forth from this time and place, to friend and foe alike, that the torch has been passed to a new generation of Americans—born in this century, tempered by war, disciplined by a cold and bitter peace, proud of our ancient heritage—and unwilling to witness or permit the slow undoing of those human rights to which this nation has always been committed, and to which we are committed today.

Let every nation know, whether it wish us well or ill, that we shall pay any price, bear any burden, meet any hardship, support any friend or oppose any foe in order to assure the survival and success of liberty.

This much we pledge—and more.

To those old Allies whose cultural and spiritual origins we share, we pledge the loyalty of faithful friends. United, there is little we cannot do in a host of new co-operative ventures. Divided, there is little we can do—for we dare not meet a powerful challenge at odds and split asunder.

To those new states whom we now welcome to the ranks of the free, we pledge our word that one form of colonial control shall not have passed merely to be replaced by a far more iron tyranny. We shall not always expect to find them supporting our every view. But we shall always hope to find them strongly supporting their own freedom—and to remember that, in the past, those who foolishly sought to find power by riding on the tiger's back inevitably ended up inside.

To those peoples in the huts and villages of half the globe struggling to break the bonds of mass misery, we pledge our best efforts to help them help themselves, for whatever period is required—not because the Communists are doing it, not because we seek their votes, but because it is right. If the free society cannot help the many who are poor, it can never save the few who are rich.

To our sister republics south of our border, we offer a special pledge—to convert our good words into good deeds—in a new alliance for progress—to assist free men and free Governments in casting off the chains of poverty. But this peaceful revolution of hope cannot become the prey of hostile powers. Let all our neighbors know that we shall join with them to oppose aggression or subversion anywhere in the Americas. And let every other power know that this Hemisphere intends to remain the master of its own house.

To that world assembly of sovereign states, the United Nations, our last best hope in an age where the instruments of war have far outpaced the instruments of peace, we renew our pledge of support—to prevent its becoming merely a forum for invective—to strengthen its shield of the new and the weak—and to enlarge the area to which its writ may run.

Finally, to those nations who would make themselves our

adversary, we offer not a pledge but a request: that both sides begin anew the quest for peace, before the dark powers of destruction unleashed by science engulf all humanity in planned or accidental self-destruction.

We dare not tempt them with weakness. For only when our arms are sufficient beyond doubt can we be certain beyond doubt that they will never be employed.

But neither can two great and powerful groups of nations take comfort from their present course—both sides overburdened by the cost of modern weapons, both rightly alarmed by the steady spread of the deadly atom, yet both racing to alter that uncertain balance of terror that stays the hand of mankind's final war.

So let us begin anew—remembering on both sides that civility is not a sign of weakness and sincerity is always subject to proof. Let us never negotiate out of fear. But let us never fear to negotiate.

Let both sides explore what problems unite us instead of belaboring the problems that divide us.

Let both sides, for the first time, formulate serious and precise proposals for the inspection and control of arms—and bring the absolute power to destroy other nations under the absolute control of all nations.

Let both sides join to invoke the wonders of science instead of its terrors. Together let us explore the stars, conquer the deserts, eradicate disease, tap the ocean depths and encourage the arts and commerce.

Let both sides unite to heed in all corners of the earth the command of Isaiah—to "undo the heavy burdens . . . (and) let the oppressed go free."

And if a beachhead of co-operation can be made in the jungles of suspicion, let both sides join in the next task: creating, not a new balance of power, but a new world of law, where the strong are just and the weak secure and the the peace preserved forever.

All this will not be finished in the first 100 days. Nor will it be finished in the first 1,000 days, nor in the life of this Administration, nor even perhaps in our lifetime on this planet. But let us begin.

In your hands, my fellow citizens, more than in mine, will rest the final success or failure of our course. Since this country was

founded, each generation has been summoned to give testimony
to its national loyalty. The graves of young Americans who answered that call encircle the globe.

Now the trumpet summons us again—not as a call to bear
arms, though arms we need—not as a call to battle, though em-
battled we are—but a call to bear the burden of a long twilight
struggle, year in and year out, "rejoicing in hope, patient in
tribulation"—a struggle against the common enemies of man:
tyranny, poverty, disease and war itself.

Can we forge against these enemies a grand and global alliance, north and south, east and west, that can assure a more
fruitful life for all mankind? Will you join in that historic effort?

In the long history of the world, only a few generations have
been granted the role of defending freedom in its hour of maxi-
mum danger. I do not shrink from this responsibility—I welcome
it. I do not believe that any of us would exchange places with
any other people or any other generation. The energy, the faith
and the devotion which we bring to this endeavor will light our
country and all who serve it—and the glow from that fire can
truly light the world.

And so, my fellow Americans: Ask not what your country will
do for you—ask what you can do for your country.

My fellow citizens of the world: Ask not what America will do
for you, but what together we can do for the freedom of man.

Finally, whether you are citizens of America or of the world,
ask of us the same high standards of strength and sacrifice that
we shall ask of you. With a good conscience our only sure reward, with history the final judge of our deeds, let us go forth
to lead the land we love, asking His blessing and His help, but
knowing that here on earth God's work must truly be our own.

In the White House

THE INAUGURATION over, President Kennedy acted quickly. He bombarded Congress with requests for legislation necessary to fulfill his pledge to get the nation moving forward. He asked for a program of expanded foreign aid and for a large defense budget. He proposed that the nation speed up its program to conquer space. He inaugurated the Alliance for Progress, designed to help nations in this hemisphere, and the Peace Corps, for helping nations in other parts of the world that wanted to help themselves.

The President constantly amazed his associates in the New Frontier by his comprehensive grasp of the nation's business and world affairs. He seemed to read every newspaper, every magazine. Officers in the Cabinet he had selected (average age 47 years) soon became accustomed to receiving short, questioning notes from the White House asking about items that had appeared but a few hours earlier in the press. The young President also began a program to increase the efficiency of the sprawling Civil Service and the General Services Administration. (Though little noticed by the public, these programs

184a

were of utmost importance to a government clogged at
every turn by unnecessary red tape.) He also did away
with the time-consuming formalities of full meetings of
the Cabinet and the National Security Council. In their
place he held informal meetings with small groups of
specialists concerned with specific aspects of foreign and
domestic policy.

As for his relationship with Congress, President
Kennedy's approach was new and personal. Frequently
he would pick up the White House phone, dial the number he wanted, and then go through a lengthy procedure,
speaking first to an answering secretary only to wait for
the Congressman he had called to come on the line. The
story quickly spread through Washington about one
recipient of such a call, who, on hearing the greeting,
"Hello, this is Jack," thought it was a practical joke and
hung up on the President.

Congress followed the young Chief Executive's lead
on foreign affairs; but it was reluctant to accept his leadership on domestic problems. The program Kennedy
wanted would require a change—in voting districts, in
associations with minority groups—and the all-powerful
little group of Southern Representatives and Senators,
who controlled the legislative committees, refused to
accept the President's solutions to the nation's problems.
This same group of Congressmen had refused in years
past to accept any suggested changes, and so, when
President Kennedy took office, it was already a time
of crisis.

The most pressing problem, civil rights, had been
building relentlessly towards a climax. The Supreme

Court, in the mid-1950's, had decreed that segregation of Negroes and minority groups was illegal. Still the law was being flaunted by many communities. Already there had been "sit-in" demonstrations and "freedom rides." As the civil rights leaders' demands increased, racial violence became more widespread. Where necessary to keep law and order— in Mississippi and Alabama—the young President called out Federal troops, in the face of opposition from those states' Governors.

The new administration had been in office only three months when it made its first major mistake. The President, acting on plans that had been initiated before he'd come into office, gave the go-ahead for Cuban exiles to invade their homeland and wrest it back from the grip of its Communist leader, Fidel Castro. Result: disaster at the Bay of Pigs. Worse, the defeat clouded the atmosphere of the summit meeting between the youthful President and Russian Premier Khrushchev that was to take place in Vienna a short time later.

Such a summit meeting (Kennedy had hoped) would provide a basis for agreement between East and West about Europe's thorniest issue, the division of Berlin. No solution could be reached at the Vienna conference. The President returned home terribly disheartened, aware that the years ahead would bring fresh crises in the Cold War. Premier Khrushchev, on the other hand, returned to Moscow mistakenly thinking the young President was weak and American leadership would collapse under increasing Communist pressure. In August, 1961, the Communists confirmed Kennedy's belief there would be trouble over Berlin. They built a Wall completely surrounding West Berlin in an attempt to stop East Berliners from crossing to the West, eventually intending to crush the Western part of the city—the section that symbolized freedom.

Despite his initial setback in Cuba, that island, only 90 miles off the Florida coast, was to provide President Kennedy with the opportunity to prove his capability to lead the Western world. The stage had been set by Khrushchev's underestimating Kennedy—the Cuban invasion had been allowed to fail, the Berlin wall had been left standing—and the Russians often openly sneered at a supposedly weak America.

So the pot built up. On Sunday, October 21, 1962, rumors swept Washington that a new world crisis was at hand. The indications were that Cuba was the focal point. It was announced that the President would speak to the nation on a matter of the greatest national urgency.

At the appointed hour, television screens across the country showed a stern and serious President. He spoke forcefully, without preliminaries, as he outlined the Communist threat against the nation: the Russians had secretly built and fortified nuclear missile sites in nearby Cuba. The danger was clear. Nuclear missiles launched from Cuban sites could knock out much of America's military strength, thereby upsetting the world's balance of power. In only 90 seconds, missiles launched from Cuba could explode in Washington. Yet only a few days earlier, the Soviet ambassador to Washington had personally assured the President that any Russian weapons being sent to Cuba were purely "defensive" in nature. The Russian ambassador had lied. The Russians were now faced with this choice, declared the President: they could either remove their missiles from Cuba and dismantle the missile sites, or the United States would be forced to take action. Meanwhile, the island of Cuba would be placed under a blockade (quarantine, he called it) by the U.S. Navy. No ships carrying arms would be allowed to reach Cuba.

It was clear that Mr. Kennedy meant what he said in this first "showdown" by an American President under threats by Russia. For five breathless days the world waited for Premier Khrushchev to react to the challenge. During these days, Kennedy prepared a military force capable of invading Cuba. Besides, thousands of bombers of the Strategic Air Command were put on constant patrol outside Russia's borders, where they could be plainly seen on Russian radar screens. American submarines carrying nuclear-tipped Polaris missiles silently cruised the waters of the world ready to strike from the secrecy of the depths. The Organization of the American States met hurriedly in Washington and, in the first unanimous action in its history, fully backed Kennedy's actions. It was known that 25 Russian ships, some bearing missiles, had been on their way to Cuba, and had not turned back!

Tension mounted. On Friday, October 26, the State Department called Russia's attention to the President's speech, especially his statement that if further work continued on the missile sites, "further action will be justified." At 9 p.m. that evening, Khrushchev admitted defeat. He sent a confused letter to Washington offering to withdraw Russian missiles from Cuba if the U.S. would guarantee not to invade the island. Then, on the following day, a second note from Moscow asked that the U.S. also pull its missile bases out of Turkey.

The administration, ignoring the proposal about Turkey, flashed word back to Moscow that we would not invade Cuba if Mr. Khrushchev would withdraw the missiles completely. The Russian leader humbly agreed. So the first confrontation of nuclear powers in history ended with a humiliating defeat for the Communists. It marked a glorious triumph for young President Kennedy —perhaps his finest hour.

Meanwhile, Kennedy was running into more domestic problems. It was a time when the administration was beginning to believe it would be able to halt the economy's steady inflationary spiral. Organized labor promised it would not seek any major wage increase in a new contract, and the administration thought business leaders would do their part by holding prices down to their current levels. But suddenly the mammoth steel industry raised its prices $6 a ton anyway. If allowed to go unchallenged, this price rise would lead to another round of increases in wages and again in prices. Fresh from his triumph on Cuba, the young President went to the mat with the barons of the steel industry. Addressing a press conference, he showed his anger. "The people will find it hard, as I do," he said, "to accept a situation in which a tiny handful of steel executives, whose pursuit of private power and profit exceeds their sense of public responsibility, can show such utter contempt for the interest of 185 million Americans."

Kennedy won his point. The steel industry backed

away from its proposed price increases. But Kennedy's anger and use of Federal pressure to win the argument sent the stock market crashing and alienated many in the business community. Big Business could not understand Kennedy's thinking that he was preventing damage to the nation's economy. The following months proved Kennedy's assessment of the situation to be correct. The nation's economy successfully weathered the threatened recession, and then turned around to score the greatest economic gains in history by adding nearly $100 *billion* to what is called the gross national product.

Still the problems of the world continued to pile upon the young President's broad and capable shoulders. The Western alliance, now that Khrushchev was no longer a threat in Cuba, was disintegrating. In France, President Charles DeGaulle was determined to make his nation a nuclear power. The British and Germans were failing to hold up their end of the NATO bargain to guard Europe with a strong military force. (At the same time, the military commitments America had made to defend Berlin had never slackened.) In Asia, Chinese Communists were trying to invade two tiny countries, Laos and Vietnam. Though small, these two nations were the key to Communist penetration of Southeast Asia. On Kennedy fell the decision to finance a preventive war in Asia. This he did, without hesitation.

Despite seemingly overwhelming problems, Kennedy also gained some substantial victories. One was the winning of broad tariff-cutting powers from a Congress afraid to put so much power in the hands of the Chief Executive. This victory meant America could take the first steps towards participating in the European Common Market. But an even greater victory—one that will probably remain the greatest monument to Kennedy's diplomacy—was the successful negotiation of a treaty with the Communists to halt tests of atom bombs and all other nuclear devices in space, within the atmosphere, and under water.

Nuclear testing had been of great concern to the administration all along. A voluntary, three-year halt (a moratorium) had been in effect when, in September, 1961, the Russians secretly exploded in Siberia the largest nuclear shots in history. Premier Khrushchev announced that one of the bombs had been equal to 50 million tons of TNT; Russian generals said the Soviet Union had developed the capability to destroy entire continents.

All this the Russians had done in defiance of worldwide appeals not to set off nuclear explosions in the atmosphere. Each bomb increased the hazards of radioactive fallout—the freeing into the atmosphere of small particles of poisonous material capable of destroying all forms of life.

It was a saddened President who had responded to the Soviet tests in 1961 by telling U.S. scientists to renew explosion of their own weapons in the air. "We have no other choice but the fulfillment of the responsibilities of the United States to its own citizens and to the security of other free nations," declared Kennedy. "We're not the ones who are important," he once remarked to a reporter. "It's the children who count for so much."

In June, 1963, the President felt the time was ripe on the atom-bomb issue to openly seek a "strategy of peace."

In a speech at American University in Washington he proposed that a first step be taken to end the vicious cycle of atmospheric testing. Negotiators led by Averell Harriman, former Ambassador to Moscow, were dispatched to Russia. A treaty was agreed to, initialed, ratified by the Senate, and put into force within an extremely short time.

Still, despite Mr. Kennedy's success in foreign policy, his problems at home were growing more critical. Leaders of the administration pointed out that the 87th Congress had passed 70 per cent of the bills the White House had asked for. This was a remarkable record; the previous administration had never been so successful. But what clouded these boasts was the unpleasant fact that a coalition of Northern Republicans and Southern Democrats still continued to hold up the most vital legislation that Kennedy sought. For the Congress, in 1961 and 1962, had rejected his proposals concerning Federal aid to public and elementary schools. It had failed to act on medical care for the aged to be financed through Social Security. It had turned down his proposal for a Cabinet department on Urban Affairs, and his plans for stiff controls of surplus farm crops.

When the 88th Congress convened in January, 1963, President Kennedy prepared to do battle again. He told the Congress there were two programs he considered "musts." One was a bill calling for sweeping civil rights legislation. The other, a program of broad tax reductions, he felt was needed as a spur to the nation's economy.

It was the new civil rights issue that changed the nation's image about the type of leader John F. Kennedy

could be. At first admirers and opponents alike had re-
garded him as a President whose primary consideration
was to be re-elected, and this meant maintaining peace
within the Democratic party, soft-pedaling the civil rights
issue, advocating caution and slow progress so as not to
cause the South to be upset. But the civil rights issue
erupted suddenly and strongly as "white supremists"
resorted to guns and bombs to deprive Negroes of their
constitutional rights and to intimidate the politicians.
Almost overnight President Kennedy became the champion of the minority groups and liberals everywhere. Indeed, his determined stand on civil rights brought him
to grips with an internal crisis more desperate than any
faced by a Chief Excutive since Abraham Lincoln.

President Kennedy met the crisis with the courage the
nation had come to expect from him. "Now the time has
come for the nation to fulfill its promise," he told the
country. "(Events) have so increased the cries for equal-
ity that no city or state or legislative body can prudently
choose to ignore them. . . . It is time to act in the Congress, in your state and local legislative body, and above
all, in all our daily lives."

Why did John F. Kennedy assume the unpopular role
of champion for a cause that could, according to his colleagues, possibly cause him to lose the next Presidential
election? One who has read this biography thoroughly
will know the answer. Another answer can be found in
his book, *Profiles in Courage*. Kennedy had written, "The
courage of life is often a less dramatic spectacle than the
courage of the final moment; but it is no less than a magnificent mixture of triumph and tragedy. A man does

what he must—in spite of personal consequences, in spite of obstacles and dangers and pressures—and that is the basis of all human morality."

John F. Kennedy fought for a strong civil rights bill, because this man did what he must. The results were as predicted. Southern Congressmen proposed to bolt his leadership. They and their "right-wing" allies in the other party began a legislative slowdown. It became apparent to all that Kennedy's major legislation, taxes and civil rights, was going to have to wait. Then, in the 1964 Presidential election, the issue could be placed once more before the public.

This then was the prospect facing President John F. Kennedy when, on November 22, 1963, he was assassinated in Dallas, Texas, a city where he had met his worst setback in the 1960 elections. It was at this point in history that a fanatic with a rifle murdered John F. Kennedy and robbed the nation of its young President.

For two years, ten months and two days, John F. Kennedy was President. It was a chill, clear sky-blue Sunday afternoon when his body was returned to the Capitol for the last time. It had been bitter cold during his inauguration, but now there was merely a chill, with the hint of winter yet to come. The scene seemed unreal.

The inaugural parade had lasted almost half a day. The mourning processions were to keep the populace glued to the television screen for most of two days.

Inside the vast, vaulted rotunda, President Kennedy's casket was placed head to the west, under the field of blue stars of the flag, on the same catafalque that had

(World Wide Photos)

One of the last pictures of President John F. Kennedy. This was taken only a few minutes before he was shot and killed by a sniper's bullet as he rode in a slow-moving motorcade into downtown Dallas, Texas. Alongside his wife Jacqueline is Governor John Connally of Texas, who was also wounded by a rifle shot.

held another President assassinated almost 100 years earlier—Abraham Lincoln. A few brief eulogies were said. Mrs. Kennedy, holding her golden-haired daughter Caroline by the hand, paced forward. Slowly they knelt by the coffin and kissed the flag that covered it. They left a President, a husband, a father to lie in state. And then the American people came to say goodbye to the man who, in doing so much for them, had given up his life.

INDEX

187